Additional

"Based on his vast ex..
Steve Becker has prov...........................guide-
book for some very dar.. territory.....area inside and
surrounding the psychopathic personality. This guide,
written non-technically, is of use to professionals of all
walks who deal with psychopaths, and to the rest of us
as well, who are potential or actual victims of a psychopath in personal or business relationships."

H. Augustus Taylor, Ph.D
Clinical Psychologist

"Steve Becker's *The Inner World of the Psychopath: A
Definitive Primer on the Psychopathic Personality* makes a
notable contribution to the literature on psychopathy.
This is a succinct, penetrating exploration executed
with a welcome lucidity.

Frank Weiss, Ph.D. *Dr. Weiss is a psychologist in pri-
vate practice in Westfield, NJ.*

The Inner World of the Psychopath

The Inner World of the Psychopath

A definitive primer on the psychopathic personality

STEVE BECKER LCSW

Disclaimer: My use of male gender pronouns in this book is for convenience's sake only. Female psychopaths exist too, if less prevalently than males. Like male psychopaths, they possess the "psychopathic mentality" that is the subject of our inquiry

ISBN-13: 9781508525110
ISBN-10: 1508525110
Library of Congress Control Number: 2015902614
CreateSpace Independent Publishing Platform
North Charleston, South Carolina

For Julia, Natalie, Leah, and Neil—my blessings.

Table of Contents

Preface

've written extensively about the psychopathic personality, also referred to as the sociopath. Between 2006 and 2012, I wrote nearly one hundred articles on this baffling, exploitative individual. I wrote most of these articles as a feature columnist for http://www.Lovefraud.com, a website founded by Donna Andersen to educate the public on psychopaths. My column afforded me the chance to explore, with great clinical freedom and creativity, my experience, observations, and perspectives on psychopaths and their victims.

In retrospect, I never expected to have as much to say about the psychopath as I did. Yet years later, my articles on "psychopathic personality" generate responses, interest, and appeals, on a regular basis, from individuals literally all over the globe, expressing gratitude for something in their experience with these destructive personalities that I've apparently understood, explained, and validated well. Routinely I hear from readers directly who seek consultation about a disturbing relationship with a suspected psychopathic individual with whom they are involved or from whom they seek escape.

My aim in this book is clear: to illuminate for the nonclinician (and anyone seeking more awareness of this personality) the **"inner world of the psychopath"**—that is, exploring his twisted machinations of thinking that lead to his breathtakingly violating behaviors. As concisely as possible, I want to leave you with a fundamental, thorough understanding of this fascinating, troubling, and troubled personality.

Early in my twenty-five-year clinical career, I developed a not-entirely welcome reputation for working skillfully with antisocial, aggressive, and manipulative male clients. More than a handful of these clients, in retrospect, had psychiatric diagnoses of narcissistic and/or antisocial personality disorders. But several of them also had the less official diagnosis of *psychopathic personality*. This predated my specific interest in this population. It was a sort of "baptism by fire" process—at the community mental health center where I worked, I became (in a sense) the *"go to"* clinician to whom many of these toughest cases were referred.

Over time, I became increasingly interested in these clients, to the point of seeking these cases over the years wherever I could (and still do). Some came (and come) to me through court mandates, others through probation departments and probation officers who saw (and see) me as receptive to, and effective working with, tough, "messy" cases.

Now and then, others have come to me through natural channels, sometimes dragged to see me, for instance, by a partner who's about to bail. In any case, that "light bulb" sometimes just goes off—that strange sense that I'm sitting with a psychopathic individual.

In the pages ahead, we will examine *who* the psychopath is, and *what* makes him psychopathic. Together, we will get *"into the heads"* of psychopaths, probing how they think and feel, and examining, in a word, the "lens" through which they experience others, themselves, and the world.

Perhaps this is a good time to note that *not* all psychopaths are men. Women can be psychopathic too, although the incidence of male psychopaths is greater than females. Still, I want to note very clearly that men have no patent on psychopathy. I stress this, at the outset, because I elect to use *male gender pronouns* throughout the book, simply to avoid the repetitive use of *he/she, he or she, etc..*

The psychopathic mentality clearly transcends gender.

I thank you, in advance, for reading my book. I hope it meets my aims and, more importantly, your expectations. And I hope to hear from you with any feedback you are willing to share. I will welcome it with gratitude.

Please note my contact information below. I also invite you to follow and subscribe to my new blog on psychopathy, where my explorations into psychopathic personality continue with regular, fresh new posts.

E-mail: powercommunicating@yahoo.com

Website: http://www.powercommunicating.com

Blog: http://www.unmaskingthepsychopath.com

Cell: 1-908-456-2679

Now, let's commence learning everything that's most important to know about psychopathic individuals.

Chapter 1

DEFINING TERMS: WHAT IS A PSYCHOPATH?
DO THE TERMS "PSYCHOPATH" AND
"SOCIOPATH" DESCRIBE THE SAME INDIVIDUAL?
DEFINING "PSYCHOPATHY" AND "SOCIOPATHY."

The terms "psychopath" and "sociopath" are often used interchangeably, and shortly we will describe and elaborate what characterizes these individuals. Presently, just know that there is no meaningful difference between the terms.

Similarly, the terms "psychopathy" and "sociopathy," less commonly referenced, also mean the same thing—referring to the condition psychopaths and sociopaths express. Think about it like this: if you were chronically and destructively reckless, and *indifferent to the impact of your recklessness* on others, we might call you a *"reckless-path"* (instead of a *psychopath*), and your condition *"reckless-pathy"* (instead of *psychopathy*).

Going forward, I am going to use the terms psychopath and psychopathy—not sociopath or sociopathy—to limit confusion.

What, Then, Is a Psychopath?

Let's start our exploration with a beginning description of the "psychopath," which we'll be expanding and deepening along the way. Above all, the psychopath is an exploitative—a *consciously violating*—individual. In his life and life history, you will find evidence of his preying and seizing upon others' vulnerabilities for his own selfish benefit.

Really it is his mentality that is psychopathic. I will spend much time emphasizing what I call the "psychopathic mentality" and furnishing clear examples of it. For the moment, we can say this: the psychopath's mentality disposes him to *chronically violating* thinking and behavioral patterns. Consequently, he hurts others, often badly and often traumatically. And yet it is *less the harm* he causes others than his *lack of accountability and remorse for the impact of his harmful behavior* that better defines his peculiarly destructive character.

I suggest that the psychopath's violating behaviors will not emerge suddenly in adulthood, as from "out of the blue." There will almost surely be a history, or suggestive history, of these tendencies dating back to childhood or certainly adolescence. Also, while the psychopath can have coexisting mental illnesses, if he is truly psychopathic, then his psychopathic behaviors will *not be caused* by another mental illness.

A core aspect of the psychopath's personality—a key theme around which much of our analysis of the psychopath will revolve—is his striking proclivity to want *what* he wants, *when* he wants it. We can infer from this that the psychopath feels entitled to *have* what he wants.

In other words, he doesn't just *want* things; he feels that he has rights to *go after* what he wants. This means that if you *have* what a psychopathic individual *wants*, you are at great risk of his targeting you to *take it* from you—whatever it might be. But the psychopath won't merely feel comfortable or justified *taking what he wants from you*; what cements his truly psychopathic tendency, as suggested above, is the *indifference he will feel* about the harm his taking from you or his violation of you causes you.

This *quality of indifference* to the *harm he inflicts* on others in the *pursuit* and *seizing* of what he wants especially characterizes the psychopath.

Chapter 2

Elaborating the Psychopath's Mind-Set—Getting inside his Mind, and How He Thinks

've already identified something very important—the psychopath is psychopathic by virtue of his psychopathic mentality. And the psychopathic mentality is defined by a combination of several concurring perspectives to which I've alluded. First, the psychopath feels a *disturbingly mindless, and often complete, entitlement* to *have* whatever it is he *wants*; further, he feels the even more alarming entitlement to *take* whatever it is he *wants* (from whomever has it). And, as I just noted above, perhaps most chillingly, he will feel an *utterly creepy detachment and indifference* to the harm of his exploitation.

For the psychopath, you (and others) *exist primarily to satisfy his gratifications.* Your *"reason for being"* or your *"function in the world"* is for *him*—specifically, it is to be (potentially) a *source* of his gratifications.

Consequently, the psychopath will tend to view you (and others) more as "objects" than as full-fledged individuals. I say "consequently" because the ramifications are big—when you view anything as an object, it becomes easier to relate to it with a *contempt for its vulnerability* and a contempt for its *right to be respected.* It becomes easier to *devalue* an "it." It becomes easier to *exploit and violate* an "it." When you view others, even animals, as objects, you are less likely to relate to them as *vulnerable beings worthy of dignity and protection.*

Hence, the psychopath looks upon the world as filled with living creatures he fundamentally views, and relates to, as objects. If you could get inside the psychopath's mind, as I will do periodically, you might find him thinking chilling thoughts like, "I got what *I* needed, and *that's* what mattered. If I had to run *you* over in the process…hey, that's because *you* were in *my* way…sorry. You *had* to be *'run over'* because you were between *me* and what I *wanted.*"

Chapter 3

FURTHER PROBING THE PSYCHOPATH'S MENTALITY

As I've suggested, the psychopath views others as *existing to meet* his gratifications. This is different from recognizing that all of us depend on others to provide us gratification. Most of us recognize this dependence without *harboring the core belief* that others *exist to gratify us* and that their sole, useful *function in the world* is to gratify us. Psychopaths, we now know, harbor this attitude.

For the psychopath, two possible scenarios tend to exist—you may *have* what he wants, or it's possible that you are *"in the way"* of what he wants. Regardless, so long as you *obstruct his access* to what he wants, he will view you as just that—an obstruction.

And because obstructions are meant to be trouble-shot, that is exactly what the psychopath does—he troubleshoots ways to neutralize your obstructive effect. He finds it simply unacceptable that you should *fail to give him* what he wants *if you have it*, or that you should *inconveniently hinder his access* to what he wants if its source should happen to lie beyond you.

The psychopath thinks things like, "You can't *stop me from having and taking* what I want. If you do, I will find a way to neutralize your opposition. *You* will *not* be the reason I fail to *get*, or *take*, what I'm eyeing. If you *get in my way*, then *you* will be primarily responsible for how I have to neutralize your hindrance."

In this way, the psychopath effectively sheds responsibility for the impact of his harm. He blames you or blames others for *"getting in his way."* I worked with a psychopathic individual who, laughingly, shared with me how he'd run right through a flock of ducks crossing the street. He ran several of them over. He was in a hurry to get somewhere. The ducks were crossing the road slowly, thereby impeding his agenda. His attitude was, *"You were in my way, stupid ducks. Oh well, that's the price you paid."*

The psychopath views people similarly. True, it's unlikely he'd run you over in the same circumstance, because he is likely to have a sense of scale. The intellectually intact psychopath will recognize, to begin with, that running you over may cause *him* less good than harm for several reasons.

Moreover, he may feel uncomfortable killing you or others (the vast majority of psychopaths aren't killers—more on that subject ahead), also for many possible reasons. Still, the analogy to the "ducks crossing the road" applies on a relative scale—that is, to the extent you impede his agenda, the psychopath will regard your rights and your right to dignity with about as much true respect as he does the ducks' right to cross the road and impede his agenda—that will be with no respect.

He will "run you over" in other ways, metaphorically speaking—sometimes with blatant violence, at other times with subtle violence—but always with a contempt for your dignity.

Chapter 4

THE PSYCHOPATH'S NARCISSISM

The psychopath is a narcissist—the most destructive type of narcissist out there. There has been controversy whether he is a "clinical species" unto himself, but there is no conclusive evidence he is. The evidence suggests more persuasively that he thinks and behaves as—that, in fact, he *is*—the most malignant of narcissists.

What is a narcissist? A narcissist is someone who possesses and acts out *extreme levels of entitlement*—someone who makes the satisfaction of his own needs so paramount and whose expectations of others to meet his satisfactions is so presumptuously imposed that he routinely abuses others' boundaries and dignity.

The narcissist tends to view others as, essentially, *mandated* to meet his satisfaction. When they don't, he will feel disappointed, which alone is not so unnatural (most of us feel disappointed when our expectations aren't met). It is *how the narcissist manages his disappointment* that is so telling. In fact, a core "red flag" of the highly narcissistic individual is the atrocious way he can be expected to deal with his disappointment. Because he feels *entitled to what he wants* and believes others *owe* him satisfaction, he is therefore outraged to be disappointed and often expresses that outrage in punitive forms, among them rage.

The narcissist's sense of entitlement is so intrinsic that, deep down, he feels he should be *spared disappointment*. He feels he is above the obligation to handle his disappointment gracefully. Instead, he licenses himself, when disappointed, to strike out, pay back, punish, and, too often, to rage. When his *needs aren't met*—and because they *tend to be insatiable, they often aren't*—he *blames others* for failing him. This makes him a *victim in his own mind*, the betrayed party, which supports his rationalizations to respond punitively.

The narcissist is disproportionately concerned with his own needs and gratifications; therefore, he is weakly interested and weakly invested in others'. Others' needs have little merit—certainly not unless and until *his* have been met.

And so you can see just how *extremely narcissistic* the psychopath is. As I've suggested, the psychopath is best understood as a *narcissist in the most extreme*. We have described his core attitudes and mentality—"It is all about what *I* want. I'm entitled to *have* what I want. Others exist to satisfy *me*. If you don't cooperate and *give* me what *I* want or *get out of my way* as I pursue my agenda, I will either *take* from you what I want or, if necessary, *move you out of my way*. And if you get *harmed in the process*, that's really *your* problem. You shouldn't have obstructed me, you fool."

This captures the alarming narcissism present in the psychopath's worldview—a narcissism impervious to self-reflection and self-correction, and a narcissism sinisterly self-rationalized. It is axiomatic to assert that *all psychopaths are pathologically narcissistic*, while not all narcissists are psychopaths.

This makes for a complex problem—how to establish, if it's even possible, the precise juncture where highly narcissistic individuals cross the *putative line* into psychopathic territory. Malignancy becomes a perhaps apt metaphor—when narcissism reaches malignant levels, disabling the capacity to view others with genuine empathy, compassion, and respect for their dignity, then it becomes psychopathic. Moving ahead, we will explore the ramifications of this.

Chapter 5

Psychopathic Behaviors in Different Presentations

Consider the short case vignettes below from clients I've worked with:

Fred is at a party and makes some jokes in poor taste about his wife, Laura She asks him to stop after the first joke, but he laughs it off and shortly cracks a second one. Now she pulls him aside and asks him, privately, to cease his ridicule, but about a half hour later he cracks a third joke, this one about her efforts to lose weight. By now, pretty much only Fred is laughing, being his own best audience. Laura feels shamed and mortified. Driving home, she confronts him in the car with his outlandish insensitivity. He says flippantly, "Lighten up, you take yourself too seriously. I was just having fun." When she confronts his flippancy, he gets angry and says, menacingly, "You know what, shut the fuck up. You are such an annoying bitch. Leave me the fuck alone."

Jim is a financial advisor and stockbroker who got himself into big trouble. He had cold-called seniors with promises of being able to turn their dwindling assets into riches, if they'd just allow him to make certain surefire, lucrative investments. He'd ask for $10,000, pretty much guaranteeing a "ten-bagger" appreciation of their investment within a year. They didn't have to do anything but just watch that $10,000 grow into $100,000, before their own eyes. Jim had no grandparents but thought nothing of telling his prospective victims that he had made all of his beloved (nonexistent) grandparents richer than they could have ever dreamed in the last five years and so wealthy that they had lots of money to leave their heirs. When a client fell for his scheme, Jim felt no remorse. Despite his intellectual awareness that he was taking money from people whose end-of-life security was fragile, his interest was purely to aggrandize himself. His attitude was basically, *"If someone is dumb enough to give me their money, I will take it gladly."* His capacity to cajole, manipulate, and con people out of their money was a separate source of satisfaction (if not thrill). He wanted the money and felt entitled to deploy his manipulative prowess to his best advantage. He neither gave thought to nor lost sleep over the complications and hardships he caused.

Richard was married and unfaithful. He was having sex with multiple women and lied with total comfort about it. When challenged with irrefutable evidence of his infidelities, he became the victim of his "accusing wife," punishing her for doubting his absurd prevarications. He denied his culpability with utter contempt, positioning his wife as paranoid and needing help. He lied to the women he slept with about his marital status, rationalizing that it was none of their business. He routinely was unprotected during his sexual hookups, conveying disregard for any risk he posed to his wife. Even after being busted for his serial, reckless betrayals, his basic attitude, as I paraphrase it, was, "Yeah, I know I shouldn't be doing this, but it feels good. I work hard; I deserve the gratification. She hasn't brought it to the table for years, so what the hell am I supposed to do? Rot my prime away just to prove I can be faithful? I'm sure she's not the angel she pretends to be. No woman can want so little sex unless she's getting some on the side, too. It's all good. When the kids get older, I'll leave her, but I'm basically just sticking it out for them."

Notice that in none of these examples are the men physically violent toward their victims. As we'll be discussing ahead, many, if not most, psychopaths are not physically violent. They victimize others in terribly violating ways, but not necessarily with physical violence.

I purposely offer these examples for their window into the psychopath's underlying mentality and attitudes that form a common denominator. You see the amazing, rationalized sense of entitlement. You see the propensity to take what they want from who has it. You see the remarkable contempt for and the baffling indifference to the harm they've caused. You see how their contemptuous devaluation of their victims supports their psychopathic dispositions. You see how chillingly unaccountable they feel for what they've done, even when faced with incontrovertible evidence of their transgressions. You see how they will try to twist blatant exposure of their guilt by *positioning the exposer* as somehow *deserving their fate*. You see how untroubled they are by deceptions and manipulations that nonpsychopaths would feel uncomfortable merely contemplating. You can see how psychopathic individuals make their amusement and their gratifications paramount, and are virtually heedless of the cost and injury to—and humiliation of—others.

I hope these brief vignettes give you a beginning flavor and a taste of the strangely disconcerting machinations psychopaths routinely deploy in the pursuit of their agendas.

Chapter 6

THE PSYCHOPATH'S AUDACITY

Psychopaths often perpetrate interpersonal (and other) violations that leave one with "Oh my God" reactions. When you are dealing with someone whose *jaw-dropping attitudes and behaviors* elicit "OMG" responses, this can be a sign that you are dealing with a psychopath.

I'm describing a quality or trait I call "audacity"—it is a quality of breathtaking daring and nerviness.

I'm not suggesting that all audacious individuals are psychopathic. They are not. Moreover audacity, like everything else, comes in degrees; it's not even the case that all *highly audacious* individuals are psychopathic. But I *am* suggesting that psychopaths—all psychopaths—*are* highly audacious. And so I see audacity as among the core traits of psychopathy.

Yet we also need to remember that it's *less a particular trait* that defines the psychopath than how—to what end—he *expresses* the trait. When audacity is expressed in forms that don't harm others or convey contempt for others' dignity, it is nonpsychopathic. The individual who *walks a tightrope between two skyscrapers* is highly audacious (and skilled). But he's impacting no one harmfully. He is risking his own welfare and no one else's with his defiant display of nerves. But the individual who *postures as a police officer to pull women off dark roads* is *psychopathically audacious*, because he's using his audacity with exploitative aims.

In their audacity, psychopaths will tend to contemplate actions that would leave the rest of us *feeling very uncomfortable or scared* as exciting challenges, less to be feared than as opportunities to display their wits, daring, and capacity to evade the most perilous cliffs of accountability.

The psychopath's grandiosity, which we'll elaborate ahead, is very much linked to his audacity. The psychopath tends to believe he can pull off pretty much anything—escape any predicament, "get over" on anyone (or any system), or dodge accountability for anything he's done, even when he finds himself cornered with no realistic escape hatches. The psychopath, in this sense, tends to perceive himself as endowed with an unlimited resourcefulness on which he can rely to extricate himself from virtually any jam.

Psychopaths tend to view themselves as having "Houdini-like" powers they experience as conferring a certain immunity from limits and accountability. In this regard, the psychopath tends to operate from a premise of his superiority that might render him shocked and, of course, outraged to fnd himself having actually been forced to "fold a deck" he believed he could play, to his advantage, indefinitely.

Chapter 7

Psychopaths As *Sometimes* Violent but *Always* Violating

There are violent, predatory psychopaths—a type of psychopathic individual that conjures up our worst nightmares. Yet not all psychopaths are violent, at least in a physical sense. Nor are all psychopaths predators in the conventional sense we tend to define predators. Moreover, not all conventionally defined predators are even psychopaths.

But if this sounds confusing, we can be sure of this: while not all psychopaths are violent, *all psychopaths, indisputably, are destructively violating*. There is a kind of violence inherent in any deeply violating attitude or behavior. And so we are talking a sensitive "fine line" when differentiating behaviors and attitudes that aren't violent in a literal sense but certainly are violent inasmuch as they harm their victims.

The Serial Killer as the Prototypically Predatory Psychopath

Serial killers are highly psychopathic, no question about it. They embody our worst nightmares of human predatory behavior. Like all psychopaths, the serial killer identifies *what* he wants and feels entitled to *take* it (in this case, *lives*).

Serial killers have had much to teach us about psychopathic attitudes and behaviors. They often exhibit psychopathic traits in extremely dramatic, frightening forms. The media naturally pays a lot of attention to these psychopaths, contributing in some respects to the false belief that most psychopaths are serial killers or are violent in predatory, homicidal ways. But this is not the case, as serial killers comprise a tiny subset of psychopaths.

Of course, psychopaths with violent dispositions and appetites are truly terrifying individuals. They will inflict violence without remorse. Some, like serial killers, will be driven by sadistic motives. Other violent psychopaths may be less sadistic, but *all psychopaths will be callous to the pain and suffering* they cause.

Which brings us back to my aforementioned client—the husband who degraded his wife at a dinner party. What relationship, if any, does he bear to the psychopathic serial killer? On the surface, it would seem challenging to find the thread that links them. But this is the thread: while the former, my client, isn't violent and murderous, as the serial killer *is*, both exhibit a *similarly chilling contempt* for their targets, whom they regard as *present for them* and as *existing for them* in the moment to exploit for the purpose of *taking their pleasure*.

More than anything, this is the mentality that captures and forms psychopathic thinking and links psychopaths of many different stripes and colors.

Chapter 8

The Psychopath behind His "Mask"

The term "psychopathic mask" refers to how some psychopaths can mask, or very carefully disguise, their exploitative agendas. Not all psychopaths are charming, smooth-talking con men (and women), but some are.

The "textbook psychopath" is a very glib (smooth-talking), persuasive individual, meaning he will mask with great effectiveness his exploitative intentions. Many of these psychopaths are charismatic and seductive, unsurprising given their generally low levels of anxiety, high levels of fearlessness, inclination to risk and adventure, and, most importantly, their perspective that others *exist to gratify them.*

I might add that psychopaths who mask well are masking several things. Most importantly, they are masking their more exploitative agendas. But if they are glib and seductive, they are also masking their emotional vapidity and superficiality, their deficient empathy, and their chilling contempt for others' dignity. There is just no avoiding that what all psychopaths are masking, *if* they are masking effectively, is ultimately their underlying, alarming emotional impoverishment.

As the psychopath observes you falling for his presentation, as he earns your trust and your belief in his mask, he may feel really good and think psychopathically, *"This is cool. This is fun. This is funny. What a fool. I've got her nailed. I am good. Look at these suckers; they're signing on the dotted line and have no idea they're not getting a damned cent back."* He may watch himself seducing another victim and pat himself on the back for possessing the power to do so.

It is easy to beat oneself up for being seduced or duped by a psychopath, especially when one has been victimized at terrible personal cost. It is easy to take the view, *"I should have seen through the psychopath's mask."* But this is being hard on oneself, especially bearing in mind that everything seems clearer in retrospect—even "red flags" we might wish we'd seen and reacted to earlier.

But it's not easy to see through people's masks. We don't, as a rule, anticipate we are dealing with people hiding behind masks that will be used intentionally to exploit us. And the reason we don't anticipate this is because it's actually the pretty rare individual who uses masks for this purpose. This seems to be largely the domain of the psychopath.

Yet it's important to point out that not all psychopaths are great maskers. Not all psychopaths are charming, glib, socially disarming, and seductive personalities. You can be psychopathic with weak or poor social skills, or even be misanthropic. Psychopaths sometimes can be forbidding and unapproachable presences, can sometimes seem ominous and disturbing, or can sometimes emit an "energy" that can leave one feeling uncomfortable or "*creeped*-out."

In a word, not all psychopaths fit the "con man" prototype. Yet enough *do* to make it worthwhile whenever we find ourselves under a sort of "spell" cast by someone, whenever we find ourselves riveted and fascinated by someone, or whenever we find ourselves overwhelmed by, or perhaps even in awe of, another's charisma, to take the proverbial step back to disengage ourselves and take stock of what's happening.

Is this individual "selling" us something? Trying to "convince" us of something? Promising us something? Are we left feeling unusually disarmed, sometimes a warning that we are in the presence of a manipulator, or possibly a seductively psychopathic individual?

Chapter 9

PSYCHOPATHS AS SMART AND DUMB BUT ALWAYS "EMOTIONALLY DEFECTIVE"

The sometimes-lingering notion that psychopaths are intellectually superior is patently a myth. There are just as many seriously dumb psychopaths out there as smart ones. But all psychopaths are seriously *emotionally deficient*—their condition is very much characterized by alarming emotional infirmities.

As just discussed, some psychopaths, paradoxically, can mask these deficiencies in the service of their exploitative agendas, but the masking doesn't negate the empty, impoverished soul beneath.

Psychopaths, therefore, fall widely across the spectrum of intellectual prowess. But in terms of "emotional intelligence" (if by this we mean, among other things, capacities for the understanding of, attunement to, and empathy and compassion for others) psychopaths (to say it very crudely) are truly, literally retarded.

It may be tougher to square this conclusion with smooth-talking psychopaths who, like puppeteers, may have honed formidable manipulative, "string pulling" skills. One can wonder—doesn't the capacity to "work people over" like that suggest a certain form of social skillfulness?

Perhaps, yes. Some psychopaths are, indeed, highly socially skillful in a manipulative sense, possessing a honed radar for others' vulnerabilities and sometimes the advanced, honed capacity to exploit those vulnerabilities.

But while some experts regard this as a form of empathy, going so far as to suggest the psychopaths' *advanced capacity for empathy* (empathy deployed destructively), I disagree strongly. I differentiate the *predatory capacity* to *size up* others' vulnerability for the *purpose of exploiting them* from the capacity to feel a true, authentic empathy, which I believe evokes an "emotional solidarity" with others that psychopaths cannot forge.

Moreover, I would argue that compassion and mercifulness are far more important measures of emotional intelligence than empathy, whose forms and definitions are difficult to specify. For instance, when a psychopath reads fear, vulnerability, doubt, or shame in someone, is he being empathetic? As I suggested, it may be true that "reading people" shrewdly is a social skill, but I don't think it meets the criterion of empathy. I think that interpersonal empathy is about reading people accurately, *responding to them with compassion and respect*, and *leaving them feeling the authenticity* of your compassionate, respectful response.

Psychopaths aren't necessarily disabled in their capacity to "read people" skillfully—as we've noted, some may possess advanced skills in this area—but their inclination to use these skills exploitatively, versus compassionately, makes them empathetically and emotionally handicapped, and dangerously so.

Chapter 10

Psychopaths are simulators of deeper emotions. As we probe what this means, let's review the matter of psychopaths and empathy. As just discussed, if by "empathy" we mean the capacity to "step into another's shoes"—to sense or know another's experience—psychopaths may not automatically disqualify. Many psychopaths, as we observed, possess a form of this capacity—the form, say, of "reading people"—keenly.

But the more important question is, how do psychopaths *use this capacity* to the extent they have it? True empathy is more than an intellectual recognition of another's experience; it is an *application of that recognition* that *connects us* with others humanely, *not* with violating, transgressive intent. By this standard, as I suggested earlier, psychopaths are grossly lacking empathy.

But this brings us to another point. If psychopaths struggle to feel real, deeper, and especially softer, more loving and connected emotions, and if they struggle to feel vulnerable emotions in a deep, authentic way, then isn't it the case, logically, that they must be simulating or somehow copying or faking these emotions to *seem* "normal" or emotionally convincing?

The answer is often, "Yes." Just as a good actor can convincingly *convey emotions* pertinent to the character he or she is playing, in the end, no matter how convincing or compelling he or she is and no matter how immersed the actor is in the role, he or she is acting. Even the greatest actors, masters at becoming "one" with their characters and the emotions their characters dictate, in the final analysis are acting.

In this sense, we might refer to psychopaths as "emotion actors," another way of saying that they do, indeed, simulate emotions--especially (as noted) the emotions that make us deeper, compassionate, empathetic, protective human beings.

Like a gifted actor who can summon any emotion called for—sadness, love, sensitivity, vulnerability, rage—the highly polished psychopath can do the same. If contrition is indicated because he's been busted again for a betrayal (and he doesn't want to lose something, like his marriage), he may be able to *convey contrition* convincingly.

Where he thinks tears are indicated—for instance, at a funeral where he feels nothing for the deceased nor empathy for the deceased's grievers—he may be able to summon tears and *seem deeply sorrowful* (whereas the nonpsychopath, even if feeling awkwardly *un*-sad, would make no effort to simulate a florid display of sadness).

Does this mean the psychopath is always in touch, consciously, with the simulated aspect of his emotional displays? I think, in general, yes, just as a great actor, "in role," no matter how deeply immersed in the role, retains an awareness that he or she is acting. But bearing in mind that psychopaths are deeply, extremely immature personalities emotionally, I think it's fair to speculate that, in certain contexts, they can *fool themselves into believing* their simulated emotional rhetoric. That is, the psychopath, in some contexts, may *buy into his own act*, so to speak, although I think this is more often the exception than the rule.

But we know that the psychopath's displays of softer emotions like remorse, regret, love, sadness, compassion, and the like will necessarily possess a shallow, simulated quality for the simple reason that there is *no place inside him* that *isn't* emotionally shallow.

Chapter 11

PSYCHOPATHS AS SHAMELESS AND SHAMING

There is nothing psychopathic per se about violating others. But when you are someone who violates others *shamelessly* and are aware you've done so, this is psychopathic territory.

Shame is usually not a good thing to be carrying around about oneself. But shame is a chastening and corrective emotion. When we've done truly shameful things—not *unshameful things* for which others are trying to shame us (an important distinction to learn to recognize)—we can learn from our shame. We feel humbled. We empathize with those we've hurt, disappointed, or transgressed; we grieve for the values we've compromised.

Shameful behaviors produce internal cataclysms—sometimes small ones, sometimes bigger ones. When we've done something shameful, we feel out of sync with *who we are*, who we value being, who we *thought* we were, and how we want others to *perceive* us (less to impress them than to restore their faith in our "truer selves" we fear we've compromised with our shameful displays).

When a nonpsychopath is busted for a serious transgression—not a traffic violation, but an act, say, of betrayal—he will feel anxious, uneasy, and *bad* about what he's done. Typically he will feel shame, guilt, and regret for the harm his actions have caused. In contrast, the psychopath *utterly lacks shame*, which renders him an emotional cipher. Now psychopaths, as we've just established, can *fake* emotions like shame (as they can attempt to fake any emotion). Recently, I consulted a couple in which the husband possessed, it struck me, clear psychopathic tendencies. He had betrayed his wife, hurting her deeply. But it was quite interesting to see him struggling to find the appropriate emotion for the occasion. He was laboring to *seem* troubled, but unable to summon up the authentic feeling. It's a strange spectacle to watch—the psychopath unself-conscious about *the self-consciousness with which he's trying to simulate emotions he's too shameless and empathetically deficient* to feel.

We can locate the psychopath's notorious lack of remorse from his *shamelessness*, because they are interconnected. When we recognize we've left someone feeling violated we feel shame, from which our remorse arises. For the psychopath, however, his missing shame, as we've established, precludes the experience of remorse.

But there is something extra troubling here, for the psychopath's very shamelessness itself engenders shame in those he harms. If it's not traumatic enough to be deeply violated, it's extra brutal to be violated by someone who betrays no remorse.

When we've been violated by another, the latter's genuine sorrow for the wound he inflicted can facilitate or even accelerate our healing. When this is missing, it can complicate or even retard one's healing process. The missing remorse is like an extra shock that must be metabolized.

Psychopaths routinely leave their victims with the *double burden* of having to heal from the original wound of their transgression and the subsequent wound of their shocking remorselessness.

Chapter 12

"To Be, or *NOT* to Be, a Psychopath"— the Psychopathic Continuum

s psychopathy a "black or white" disorder, meaning you are either a psychopath or not one at all? This is a tricky question, with experts in some disagreement on the answer.

In most areas of life, most of us fall on continuums and spectrums of various conditions, tendencies, and behaviors. Take "anger management." Some of us would measure quite low in expressions of *poor anger management*; others would fall somewhere in the middle, managing our anger reasonably well, perhaps occasionally less well; while others of us might tend to *manage our anger poorly* more frequently, and well less frequently.

This is also the case with psychopathy, to an extent. There are various scales that measure psychopathic traits and tendencies. Most of us would rate quite low on these scales, meaning we'd possess very few psychopathic traits. Others of us might rate somewhere in the middle, possessing some psychopathic traits but in somewhat attenuated (weakened) forms, meaning that certain tendencies might be evident but unlikely to be expressed in chronic, extremely destructive ways. But higher up on the psychopathic scales, we'd locate those individuals who possess psychopathic qualities to a more extreme degree, who can be *counted on* to behave quite often in violating, transgressive ways.

It's true, then, that determining *precisely where* on any psychopathic scale we establish a cutoff—below which we designate all nonpsychopaths and above which we designate all psychopaths—may possess a certain arbitrary, imprecise quality.

Robert Hare, Ph.D., has developed what are regarded as the most clinically valid instruments to rate psychopathy levels in individuals. Hare's assessment tools extensively evaluate both an individual's psychology and behavioral history. His PCL-R (Psychopathy Checklist, Revised) scores people from zero to forty, designating those scoring above thirty to be flat-out psychopaths, while deeming those falling below thirty to be incrementally less and less psychopathic the farther below thirty they score.

Still, I think it's important to exercise caution in approaching the question whether psychopathy is a relative—versus a *more absolute*—personality orientation. It may be best to move away, in certain circumstances, from metrics and scale numbers and to remind ourselves we are not talking about capacities to be hurtful, insensitive, cruel, self-centered, or deceptive, for these are common capacities.

To be psychopathic, we are talking about *incapacities*--for instance, the incapacity to be empathetic, compassionate, truly guided by conscience, protective from love and loyalty toward others. Moreover, as we just discussed, we're talking about the incapacity to be chastened by shame, from which deep, genuine experiences of remorse arise.

This is really what defines the psychopath—less his capacity to think and behave badly than his incapacity to feel deeply disturbed by this capacity.

Chapter 13

CAN PSYCHOPATHS BE TREATED?
CAN THEY CHANGE?

The psychopath is not treatable and he won't change, certainly not from self-awareness or the awakening of a conscience that is missing. Expecting the psychopath to change is like expecting a totally deaf person someday to hear.

Psychopaths, in fact, are "emotionally deaf" in the ways we've been elaborating. Self-centeredness that goes as breathtakingly deep into character as the psychopath's simply precludes the confrontation or the true examination of itself. Therefore, we can say confidently that the psychopath's mentality is immutable or unchangeable.

After all, what is the basis of self-change, especially self-change in regard to how we mistreat others? To begin with, you have to *care about how you hurt others* and how you leave them feeling violated. Well, we can disqualify the psychopath at the starting line for, as we've stressed repeatedly, his peculiar condition—the essence, really, of his condition—is simply *not to care how he harmfully impacts others.*

The psychopath lacks another quality basic to the process of self-change—the capacity to feel mortified by the worst things we do. When we step back to contemplate, with mortification, the damage our selfishness, cruelty, and self-centeredness have caused, this can be a game changer. This can "wake us up" to the need to *become who we thought we were*, to realign us with our concept of ourselves.

But the psychopath doesn't awaken to this experience; he feels no self-horror. He is not prone to the internal "quake" that arises from the consciousness of a blatant discrepancy between our self-concept and our behavior. For the psychopath, insufficient *psychological dissonance* is present to arouse alarm about himself; hence, he lacks the intrinsic motivation to change. Where there is *"no shame, expect no gain."* The psychopath's shamelessness, as we discussed earlier, assures his incapacity to evolve or reform into a more substantial individual.

There is evidence that the psychopath "burns out" with age, suggesting his psychopathic behaviors decrease over time. To the extent this is so, it can be attributed not to his genuine personal growth or a true shift or alteration of his psychopathic mentality, but more likely to *diminishing reserves of energy* deployable for psychopathic expression.

But make no mistake—the psychopath will always *feel* and *think* like a psychopath, even if he tries to suggest or contrive that he's evolved. While his production of psychopathic behaviors might subside as he edges past middle and into old age, his mentality won't change a bit—of this you can be sure.

Chapter 14

Estimates vary concerning the incidence of psychopathy in the general population. Some are clearly overblown: writers like Martha Stout, PhD, suggest that upward of 4 percent of the general public is psychopathic. This seems a reckless figure that far exceeds the true numbers.

Robert Hare, PhD, identifies that figure as something just below 1 percent of the general population. This seems a far more accurate and responsible estimate, pertaining to individuals considered to be highly psychopathic, not those with mild or moderate psychopathic tendencies. Perhaps the experts suggesting figures in the 4 percent area are carelessly including individuals with psychopathic tendencies who would not meet criteria for the designation of full-blown psychopath.

Most prisoners are not psychopaths, and the vast majority of psychopaths are not in prison. It is also the case that the vast majority of criminals and criminal mentalities are not in prison.

In other words, like it or not, the vast majority of people who do bad things; who hurt, violate, and sometimes ruin others; and who transgress rules, laws, and boundaries in outrageous ways are *not* presently locked up. Only a very small percentage of them are—for the pretty basic reason that most of them aren't caught or reported. And among those who are and who have to pay a legal consequence for their transgressions, few of these individuals end up in prison. But even when they do, most of these offenders are likely to get released from prison sooner than later; in all probability, even these individuals are *not* in prison as we speak.

Yet of those imprisoned, how many are truly psychopathic? Here I tend to trust Hare's estimates, which suggest something neighboring in the 20 percent range. It might seem surprising that something close to 80 percent of prisoners would fail to qualify as full-blown psychopaths despite their having committed crimes serious enough to land them in prisons.

So how do we explain this? Why isn't more of the prison population psychopathic? This is a good question, but before answering it, let's keep in mind several things worth noting. While it's true that the vast majority of psychopaths are not in prisons, and most never end up in prison, the *percentage of psychopaths* represented by the prison population far exceeds that of the general population. Remember, something just less than 1 percent of the general population probably qualifies as psychopathic, while upward of 20 percent of the prison population does.

We are not saying, then, that prisons house fewer psychopaths than the general population because prisoners are less likely to be psychopathic than the general population. That would not be the case, because prisoners are much more likely to be psychopathic as a sample group against the general population. The problem is simply that prisons house such a small component of all the criminally minded and criminally behaved individuals out there that, on the whole, they do not protect us very well from the millions of psychopaths, most of whom evade prison and many of whom, seeing prison time, are released. But still, it's a fair question—why aren't more prisoners psychopathic? For the answer, we return to what is the *essence of psychopathy*—remembering that it is a particular mentality.

Many prisoners—again, perhaps 75–80 percent of them—simply lack purely psychopathic mentalities. They tend to fall into the category of individuals who've done bad, wrong things and committed serious crimes, but who've done these things typically with *nonpsychopathic mentalities*.

Gang-related crimes, drug-related crimes, and even many violent robberies are often perpetrated less with exploitative motives than in conjunction with sub-cultural factors, laws, and lawlessness. Sub-cultural violence is often sowed in poverty. Factors of desperation—for survival, security, status, and affiliation—play a role in much criminal activity that lands people in jails and prisons.

Consider briefly two prisoners. One is a nineteen-year-old gangbanger who shot and killed a rival gang member in a drive-by shooting. It was considered a retaliatory killing on the tough streets of Plainfield, NJ. This young man killed with a sense of ambivalence. He was caught, charged, and convicted, and finds himself doing time in a maximum-security prison in New Jersey. He did not sleep well the night he killed. He was overwhelmed with a mixture of excitement and a certain surreal giddiness from the power of having taken a life, but also with fear and a certain shock and underlying unease at having done so. Later, he broke down when interrogated by detectives and confessed.

Now he is in prison for a long time. This young man is not atypical of many inner-city males in prison—he is a nonpsychopathic killer who killed as a function of his loyalty to a gang and in a context of sub-cultural violence. He killed with ambivalence in the aftermath of which, despite his initial front of toughness and sto-icism, he felt troubled by what he'd done.

Contrast this with another prisoner, a forty-five-year-old white male, who fraudulently posed as a financial advisor and broker, swindling his clients out of close to $400,000. He too was arrested and convicted, and is doing time. He felt no ambivalence *posturing* as someone he wasn't nor the least bit of guilt taking his trusting clients' money with no in-tention of returning it to them. He was not part of anything like a sub-culture of poverty, desperation, and violence. Rather, he was a lone, greedy wolf tar-geting vulnerable victims because he *wanted money*, was *greedy for money*, and believed that if he *could find people dumb enough to entrust their money to him*, he was *entitled to take it*.

Let me repeat this, because it captures the essence of the psychopath's mentality and the central focus of our examination. The financial con man's thinking was classically psychopathic: *"If I can find people dumb enough to give me their money, I'll take it. It's almost funny how easy it is to find these suckers. Jesus, I'm good. I'm really* *fucking good. People are so stupid. They will believe anything. Is what I'm doing right? Who cares if it's right? Right or not, I'm $400,000 richer. That's the beauty of America, the land of opportunity."*

Two prisoners: the first a nonpsychopath who murdered; the second, a text-book psychopath who murdered no one but devastated lives with the blithe attitude of one playing a practical joke.

Chapter 15

t is difficult to pinpoint precisely the relative contribution that nature and nurture make to the development of psychopathy. Yet it seems almost certain that psychopaths have a biological predisposition to becoming psychopaths. And considerable research has postulated various differences in psychopaths' brains that could account for their *psychopathically aberrant* behaviors. Yet a definitive identification of *biological causes* of psychopathy remains elusive.

So the answer to the question, *"Are psychopaths born or raised?"* seems inconveniently complex. Probably some individuals are so *strongly biologically predisposed* to psychopathy that even the most favorable, nurturing upbringings would fail to prevent its eventual emergence. In others, a richly nurturing upbringing might divert a predisposition to psychopathy into more *pro*social—that is, less *anti*social—expressions.

And yet a great many psychopaths, perhaps a majority, had childhoods—if their histories were carefully assessed—that failed to optimally counteract or neutralize psychopathic predispositions and risk factors. I refer to childhoods characterized by poor parental role models, weak (if not missing) opportunities to form secure attachments, and exposure to neglectful, abusive, and/or traumatic experiences that would have limited the aforementioned opportunities to redirect or sublimate any psychopathic potential.

I'm suggesting, too, that psychopathic traits alone don't *make the psychopath*. Something more than traits themselves must contribute to a *fuller development* of psychopathy or *any* character disorder. More important than traits themselves are the *forms of expression* they take.

Take, for instance, an individual with highly manipulative tendencies. Not all manipulation is destructive. Suicidal individuals can be manipulated off high bridges. That is not a psychopathic expression of manipulation, quite obviously. Similarly, hijackers and kidnappers can be expertly manipulated to release innocent hostages—a constructive use of manipulation. We use forms of manipulation constantly to convince and influence each other, often with positive intentions. And so the trait *"manipulativeness"* doesn't implicate someone as psychopathic. It is *how the psychopath expresses manipulation* (and other traits) to *support his exploitation* that captures the essence of his condition.

Consider an appetite for high risk, also associated with the psychopathic mentality. This is a trait well suited to performing many unnerving, even heroic behaviors that most of us would actively avoid. But when an *appetite for risk* is used in the service of *audaciously exploiting others*, then the trait is being *deployed psychopathically*.

I've deviated slightly from the original question, *"Are psychopaths born or raised?"* I've suggested that some individuals really would appear to be *"born psychopaths,"* while others' paths to psychopathy are likely to have been less predestined, cases of predispositions meeting childhoods that, unfortunately, supported those predispositions.

You look at certain textbook psychopaths, like Ted Bundy, and find yourself reasonably speculating that this man was *born with a psychopathic darkness* that, inevitably, would have emerged in violent and perverse forms *under any circumstances*. Of course this can't be proven, yet one senses it to be true. This isn't to say that Bundy himself had anything close to an optimally nurturing childhood. Evidence suggests the contrary despite Bundy's idealistic representation of his upbringing in his preexecution interview, in which he denies its pathological aspects that are consistent with his lifelong pattern of manipulation, deception, and perhaps self-deception.

Yet still, when you consider a Ted Bundy, you remain struck, to be sure, with a sense that, even had he been raised in an optimal environment, the psychopathic forces within him seemed destined for devastating expression. Conversely, I think it's fair to speculate that individuals born with *little to no psychopathic predisposition* are unlikely to evolve into fullblown psychopaths. After all, this must explain why so many millions upon millions of individuals, across decades and centuries, who were subjected to the most heinous childhood neglect, while not unaffected or untraumatized, did not (and generally, do not) become psychopaths.

Chapter 16

A NARCISSIST OR PSYCHOPATH? WHO AM I DEALING WITH?

Let us probe a bit more deeply into a subject we examined more generally in Chapter 4, addressing the challenging question of differentiating the psychopath from the nonpsychopathic narcissist.

Psychopathy can be viewed (as many view it) as a *disorder of narcissism* or, as I might suggest, as *"narcissism gone wild"* (that is, narcissism exhibited in its most virulent form). The psychopath might be seen as the cousin the narcissist is *warned he is becoming* and better watch himself before it's too late. This isn't to say that the highly narcissist individual is greatly more amenable to treatment than the psychopath—just that the farther up the "scale of narcissism" we climb, as we find ourselves entering psychopathic territory it's safe to say that all bets are off, meaning *hope of change* is futile.

Underlying all disordered expressions of narcissism is a problem of *entitlement*—we might say, *"Entitlement gone wild."* Consequently, when you are dealing with a significantly narcissistically disturbed individual, you can be absolutely certain that the individual before you, if nothing else, harbors—however well-concealed— levels of entitlement that are flat-out malignant.

So what differentiates the narcissist from the psychopath?

In general, the psychopath violates others *as a pattern* with a *more complete indifference to the harm he causes* than your typical narcissist does. As we've stressed at length, psychopaths will exploit others with callous indifference, with "void" consciences, whereas a narcissist, capable of inflicting interpersonal harm in a multitude of chronic, destructive ways, is less likely to do so with quite the psychopath's chilling equanimity. The narcissist might not lose much sleep over his harmful impact, but he might lose just a little or find his sleep just a bit restive, even if he's puzzled why. Conversely, the psychopath, rest assured (no pun intended), will sleep as undisturbed as if he performed a mitzvah earlier in the night.

The narcissist will likely have a greater need than the psychopath to rationalize the abusive expression of his entitlement—for example, his entitlement to rage, demand, and control, and to seize his gratifications. Unlike the psychopath, his conscience may be *"missing in action"* but may not be *totally missing*. To the extent it's not entirely missing, the narcissist has to "make it go away" so he can pursue his agenda unencumbered by a conscience that may *just be beating audibly enough* to gnaw at him under the surface.

The psychopath is less encumbered, lacking even a *suppressed conscience* to confront—it is missing entirely, and thus poses no obstruction to his exploitative agenda.

There comes a point along the narcissist continuum where the distinction between the two is virtually meaningless. High enough up on the continuum, the narcissist has become highly psychopathic and is now a psychopath. We have a pretty clear sense where that *mentality marker* on the continuum lies—it lies at the point where the narcissist no longer struggles, even subconsciously, with his mortifying violations. Now he is psychopathic and extra, chillingly menacing.

None of this is to suggest a favorable prognosis for the individual with a narcissistic personality disorder. The prognosis is very poor. Empathetic and compassionate deficits are grievous, if not fatal. Contempt for others' needs wields itself again and again with terrible impact. Vertiginous vacillations between the idealization and devaluation of others wreak confusion, pain, and havoc. The narcissist's self-centeredness and entitlement are so great as to preclude, generally, meaningful self-awareness. Perhaps an intellectual-based self-awareness may be present, but it will lack the self-alarm that propels us toward the hard work of meaningful personal growth.

If you were to seek a silver lining of hope with some—not all, but some—very disturbed narcissists, it refers to what we alluded above. Their *consciences* may be beating weakly but are somewhere beating. Deep down, they may suffer disquiet over the havoc they cause. They may not like themselves for who they are, and they may even loathe themselves. They may recognize they have personality demons and, in rare cases, choose to examine them. But I'm talking rare cases. These are not individuals from whom to expect this.

Psychopaths, however, have none of these underlying *demons of conscience* to fight. When the narcissist exploits someone for his gratification, he may have to *convince himself* (on a deeper level) that his victim deserved it. (This is his *conscience's damage-control mechanism* in action.) The psychopath won't have to expend the energy to convince himself. His victim *will have deserved it* merely for the fact that she was exploitable.

The psychopath sees things along these lines: if you are vulnerable to exploitation or *make yourself* vulnerable to exploitation, then he isn't to blame for exploiting your vulnerability. *You* are to blame for *making yourself vulnerable*.

For the psychopath who steals $50,000 of your money "to invest," in his mind this is tantamount to your having *volunteered to just hand him the money*. In his warped mind, it's as if you just *gave it to him*. Sure, he knows, intellectually, that he cajoled it from you, but psychologically he will process it as though you ended up just *giving it to him*. For the psychopath, what you are vulnerable enough to have *taken from you* is synonymous with your *handing it to him*—even if what he takes from you is with force.

Chapter 17

Can Psychopaths Love?

Because psychopaths are emotionally shallow, with gaping deficits of empathy, compassion, and true loyalty, it is safe to say that, at best, they can *simulate experiences of love* but lack a capacity to love genuinely and certainly deeply.

Psychopaths love neither others nor themselves. Love is just not a factor or experience in the psychopath's world. Psychopaths can crave things, but to love a human being means possessing the capacity to sacrifice for that individual from the heart, not from expedience. When psychopaths sacrifice, it's not from a deep interest to give of themselves, risk their welfare, or forsake their gratification for the true benefit of another or even a cause.

Something else is driving them—there is something *"in it"* for them, which may or may not be obvious. Take the ISIS terrorist who makes videos of his beheading of captives. He is a psychopath without question. The cause to which he dedicates himself becomes a *medium for the expression of his psychopathy*. His loyalty to ISIS is less important than using his affiliation with ISIS to channel his psychopathy.

Psychopaths can be effective at finding vehicles, even affiliations with groups or movements, that offer them opportunities and outlets to express their psychopathy. The psychopath is loyal, in the truest sense of loyalty (risking real sacrifices to his own self-interests), to no one. So long as his "loyalty" benefits him, he may appear ardently and inspirationally reliable, like someone you'd want in a trench with you. But jeopardize his interests, and watch out—he will *slit your throat* in that trench or give you up. He will sacrifice *you*, not *himself*, in the blink of an eye, his mind-set being, *"That's the way it goes. Somebody's ass needed to be saved. Why should it have been yours? Sorry, but really not. That's life."*

The psychopath's disloyalty isn't episodic, or about instances here and there of disloyalty strewn across a lifetime. Neither is it about his *capability of disloyalty* but rather about his *incapability of loyalty*—especially, as just noted, his incapability of loyalty when he stands to really *give up something important* to remain loyal. To reiterate, facing this predicament, the psychopath will *throw you under the proverbial bus* every time, no matter who you are and who you were, no matter how far back you go, and no matter how important you thought you were to him. Facing real sacrifice, he will sacrifice *you* every single time.

Therefore, psychopaths do not feel love in the deeper sense of what it means to feel love. This isn't to say that love isn't a complex, arguable construct itself, with many shades, nuances, manifestations, and shifting intensities. For this reason one could object, "How can you say that psychopaths can't feel 'love' when love itself is arguably such an imprecise, elusive concept?"

My response to this intelligent retort is, whatever "love" is arguably, however elusive its meaning, and however subjective its experience, psychopaths aren't feeling it on a deep level at all toward anyone—not for their wives, their mothers, or their children.

Chapter 18

THE PSYCHOPATH'S GRANDIOSITY

The psychopath is a highly grandiose personality. He typically feels he can get away with anything. This doesn't mean he is necessarily entirely delusional about his skill set in this respect; he may, in fact, be highly practiced and polished as an effectively scheming manipulator.

But there's a big difference between confidence and grandiosity, and the psychopath is typically much more than confident—as stated, he is highly grandiose. That said, while part and parcel of the psychopath's mentality, grandiosity itself doesn't make him psychopathic. It is the *expression his grandiosity takes* that characterizes, with the expression of various other tendencies and traits, his psychopathic mentality. The psychopath sees himself as *Houdini-like*. Trap him, bust him, or drive him into a corner, no matter; he expects to prevail unscathed.

The psychopath's grandiosity is best expressed in his underlying faith that there is virtually *no limit* to what he can get away with. However advanced a manipulator he may really be, his grandiosity propels him to greater and greater risks, in a flaunting of his contempt for others' boundaries and dignity. Also, his grandiosity will rarely be deployed toward prosocial aims—believing, for instance, that he, unlike all those other "idiot researchers," will be the first to find a cure for Alzheimer's disease. Rather, his grandiosity is far more likely to be deployed for purposes of exploitation.

Moreover, in his grandiosity, the psychopath doesn't merely see himself as superior but others as inferior. He isn't just a brilliant, master manipulator—others *are stupid*, their relative stupidity making them *deserving targets* of his exploitation. He isn't just fearless and willing to tackle high-risk challenges—others are cowards, pathetic, and lower than he for their disinclination to court the risks he will.

This is where the psychopath's contempt for and devaluation of others are so evident and intrinsic to his "self" and "other" worldview. It is not unusual to see a psychopathic individual attempting to suppress the glint of a smile when confronted with having violated someone whose forgiveness he seeks. Alluding again to this shamelessness, I've seen a psychopath grab, *as if* tenderly, the hand of a spouse he's blatantly betrayed and apologize for the betrayal (likely executed in the grandiose belief that he'd never be exposed) with the glint of a smile discernible beneath the veneer of his contrived remorse. In these moments you are witnessing not only his *simulated summoning* of emotions, but also the display of his grandiosity—that cocky look he can't always fully disguise that belies a confidence in his insuperable powers to finesse his way out of any bind.

For even in a moment of great tension, as he ostensibly comforts the person he's violated in a seeming ownership of his treachery, one has the sense he is thinking, self-consciously, *"I'm doing great. All I have to do is play this game of contrition and comforter, and I'll be fine again with her in no time."*

Which brings us next to the psychopath's strange belief in his immunity to accountability.

Chapter 19

THE PSYCHOPATH'S "IMMUNITY MENTALITY"

Psychopaths, as a byproduct of their grandiosity, tend to feel a strange immunity to the ramifications of their transgressions. I call this their "immunity mentality."

Most of us, even on the lowest moral plane of thinking, when contemplating a violating or perhaps seriously illegal act, will be deterred by thoughts like:

"I *could* get caught, and if I do, I could be *screwed*."

"What *if* I get caught? If I get busted, I'm *really* up shit's creek. And I'll *deserve* to be. Of course, I may *not* get caught, but I'm *taking a big risk*, and *big consequences* come with it. Let me *think twice*."

Even, as I say, at this lowest tier of moral calcula-
tion, psychopathic individuals do not tend to think like
this. Psychopaths expect to escape the consequences of
their audacious transgressions. Intellectually, they will
register the possibility that they could get caught, but
on a psychological level, with their *reckless, grandiose
confidence*, they expect *not* to.

Some are too impulsive-minded to think beyond
executing the act that seizes their imagination. Others
may contemplate an agenda somewhat more seriously.
In either case, two factors are almost assuredly at play,
factors to which I've alluded like a chorus throughout:
the shocking lack of concern for the harm their action will cause, and their almost surreal assumption,
steeped in their grandiosity, that they will "get over"
on whoever they are exploiting.

Psychopaths just don't suffer deeply the worry of
apprehension; it's as if they carry, as suggested, the protection of an *"immunity card"*—a sense of immunity
steeped in their grandiosity. But even *should* they get
caught, psychopaths are hardly likely to dissolve into
panic. This is unsurprising given their aforementioned
inordinately high levels of confidence that they will finesse their way out of virtually any predicament.

Yet still, the psychopath's peculiar equanimity facing seemingly inevitable exposure and impending, serious sanctions is quite striking. Surely most psychopaths

have been busted for their exploitative behaviors, whether on personal levels, job/career levels, or legal/ criminal levels. Wouldn't a prior history of having been busted leave them extra concerned about the *real risks* of being busted in the present and future?

Psychopaths are far *less* risk averse than nonpsychopaths. In other words, psychopaths seem to have a *higher risk tolerance* than is usual. Consequently, they may *seek and need risk* to "feel alive" and possibly to compensate for propensities to feel bored and understimulated. For the psychopath, a high-risk act that would shake a nonpsychopath's equilibrium to the core may actually have an *equilibrium-restoring* effect, taking him from an *"out of sorts"* state of mind to a more *satisfied feeling*.

But returning to the chapter's theme. psychopaths seem to possess a view of themselves as virtually *immune to* or *cloaked in protection* from the ramifications of their shenanigans. Where others shudder at the thought of having to account for transgressions, the psychopath is unfazed. He does not expect to have to "face the music," but when he does, he often retains his strange, often glib equanimity.

Watching a psychopath being grilled as a suspect, say, in a murder, you might have the impression that he's engaged in a discussion of a traffic offense, not his suspected involvement in a homicide.

Chapter 20

PSYCHOPATHS AS ABUSERS

Although it is true that a high percentage of abusive individuals are not psychopathic, and also true that not all psychopaths are "classically abusive" in relationships, many psychopaths are, in fact, extremely abusive personalities and sometimes very dangerously so.

When we refer to individuals as abusive personalities, we are referring to those who express various forms of bullying, controlling, intimidating, coercive, punitive, and exploitative attitudes and behaviors toward others *as a pattern*.

Abuse is often misunderstood to be essentially an anger management problem, when its central essence is a mentality—the "abusive mentality."

The abuser's mentality, not surprisingly, is a highly narcissistic and, perforce, highly entitled one—a mentality that subscribes deeply to the underlying belief that "others *must cooperate* with me, others must *not* disappoint me, and others *must conform* to my expectations, or else I *will punish them*. I will punish them for disappointing me and defying me, or sometimes I will punish them just because I'm frustrated as hell *and someone needs to be punished*."

Some abusers abuse in a slathered rage, while others abuse with sadistic, composed contempt. Abuse, as we know, can take multiple forms—verbal and physical being the most commonly emphasized. But it's possible to abuse someone nonverbally, as well. For instance, refusing to talk to someone, refusing to acknowledge their concerns, refusing to process a conflict with them, or watching them twist in the wind from your stonewalling attitude—these, too, are forms of abuse.

Underlying abuse in all its forms is the *exploitative imposition of control* over someone *perceived to be vulnerable and, to some extent, defenseless*.

The psychopath, among many things, is an abusive personality. His abusiveness may or may not be effectively disguised. He may fit the profile of a dangerous, terrifying domestic abuser, but not necessarily. Many psychopaths, as I noted above, aren't classic domestic abusers.

But we know that somewhere in his life the psychopath has abused, is likely presently abusing, and is at *high risk of perpetrating an impending abuse*. He is almost certain, at any given time in his life, to be abusing someone's trust and/or boundaries. If he is not abusing individuals, the psychopath is abusing rules, boundaries, systems, or laws, with the hallmark contempt of the abuser.

The psychopath, as I've stressed repeatedly, is *as if programmed* to "get over" on others. He is an exploiter deep in his DNA (physiological and/or psychological), and *exploitation is always abuse*. Moreover, he is a *remorseless abuser*. Not all abusers are remorseless; to be sure, remorse for one's abuse—relative or retroactive—never mitigates the harm of the abuse. This is especially true inasmuch as abusers, remorseful or not, will repeat their abuse unless and until they seek serious help for it.

Psychopaths, though, happen to be remorseless abusers. Their expressions of contrition, if present, will be shallow, manipulative, and self-serving. They will be intended to preserve *their* security, not address in a meaningful way how they've shattered *yours*.

This bears elaboration. The psychopath may express contrition, and glib psychopaths may seem highly convincing in their expression of it. Some psychopaths, as we've addressed, can produce even softer emotions on cue, like terrific "method actors" summoning such emotions to fit their manipulative aims.

But the psychopath's apologies, expressions of remorse, contrition, or regret are assuredly shallow, transitory, superficial displays driven by present self-interest. He may have many reasons to seek his way back into your good graces, but none of them will be deep or from remorse, or impel him to seriously examine himself.

Remembering that what defines the abusive individual is much less his *poorly managed anger* per se than a mentality that sees others as *targets for the exploitative imposition of his power*, we can assert confidently that psychopaths embody the abusive mentality.

We can be equally confident that the psychopath is incapable of owning and resolving his abuse on a deeper level (as a minority of nonpsychopaths can do) for the regrettable reason that he is psychopathic.

Chapter 21

THE PSYCHOPATH IN THERAPY

t's probably worth stating again, clearly, that psychopaths are not individuals who can be helped. When
psychopaths end up in the therapist's office, the best-
case scenario is that the therapist recognizes he is dealing with a possibly psychopathic individual, and sooner
than later terminates the therapy.

Psychopaths will show up from time to time in
therapy, almost never voluntarily, but when voluntarily,
undoubtedly with an ulterior motive. Psychopaths,
true to their general modus operandi, will be trying to
"get over" on the therapist they are seeing. They may
seem cooperative and possibly somewhat convincing
that they're motivated to make meaningful changes;
they may seem, even, convincingly to own some

things. But it will all be a pretense, a facade, a form of gamesmanship.

The desperate belief that *if* only your psychopathic partner or loved one would be willing to get help, *then* there is hope--this is an understandable, but delusional, position. Even if your psychopathic loved one is willing to see a therapist or enter a program, it will be from a selfish agenda, not from a genuine intention to make meaningful use of the available resources. He will be wasting others' time to buy himself your forgiveness, or your extra tolerance of his past and future antics, or more rope with which he'll end up hanging *you*, not himself.

The psychopath in the therapy setting, just as in public settings, doesn't make a singular or singularly identifiable presentation. He may be court-mandated and possibly transparent in his disinterest to be present. He may be *"wife-mandated"* and equally candid about his cooperative but less than highly motivated agenda to be present. Or, as noted, he may display a more voluntary facade, purporting more sincere ambitions, with no genuine intent or capacity to actualize them.

In a couples therapy format, same deal—many partners of psychopathic individuals find hope on the basis of their psychopathic partner's willingness to attend couples therapy, sometimes even cooperatively. But often this is a function of the psychopath's having been busted for deceptive behaviors or big lies and finding himself on the brink of losing a relationship that confers too many conveniences to be *"worth losing."* Hence, his presence in therapy often is to mollify his outraged, mistrustful partner, to forestall her flight.

The psychopath in couples therapy is incapable of doing meaningful work on a relationship because he is incapable of deeply valuing a relationship or his partner. It's also inadvisable to do couples therapy with psychopaths or any abusive individual, given their relatively high risk of using session material to punish their partners outside the sessions.

There is no science to establishing quickly and with certainty that you are dealing with a psychopath clinically, but there are certain experiences of these personalities that are revealing to a sensitive clinician. To begin with, many psychopaths do not mask their glibness very well, and I find that *early exhibits of glibness* can be especially suggestive of psychopathic tendencies. It is one thing to be glib—to be a charming, disarmingly smooth-talking individual. But to reveal one's glibness quickly, or almost immediately, suggests not just glibness but that quality of audacity so characteristic of the psychopath.

One can feel somewhat startled by these prematurely glib displays, whose manifest intent can appear benign, friendly, and congenial; in absorbing them, however, one is left with the feeling of having just been slightly invaded, as though a liberty was taken too soon.

Contrary to myths about psychopaths, I think that many of them do a rather poor job of masking their emotional superficiality. One can sometimes feel a jarring, palpable disjunction between the psychopath's *projected experience* of himself and one's *actual experience* of him. This returns us to the territory of his simulation of emotions. For instance, one can be sitting with a psychopath, as noted above, who may be striving to convey a feeling of remorse and regret, and who may even summon tears—yet his emotional displays may have an *apocryphal feel* to them. The psychopath can *feel apocryphal* to be with.

I drift a bit from the main point—that the psychopath in therapy is a futile concept. If you are fortunate enough to suspect or know that you are dealing with a psychopathic individual, the recommendation isn't to refer him to a therapist. What, then, is the best recommendation? Let's consider this next.

Chapter 22

I'm Dealing with a Suspected Psychopath—Now What?

There is only one thing to do when you suspect or know you are dealing with a psychopathic individual, and that is to *run for the hills* and personally own, understand, and resist all the gravitational pulls back toward this individual.

Many experts have had their say about this at length, but it belongs in this primer. The psychopath with whom you are involved will never change, and any and all hope you have that he will is misguided. Although he is not *always acting psychopathically* and *sometimes acts nonpsychopathically*, he is *always still a psychopath*, will *always think* like a psychopathic, and, predictably or not, inevitably will *periodically exploit your trust and vulnerability*.

Escaping from dangerous, violent, vindictive psychopaths requires more careful consideration of, and also consultation with (and the accumulation of), resources for support and safety. But there is nothing wise to do except *leave psychopathic individuals with unequivocal conviction* and, as I've noted, to confront all the insidious, powerful forces that can tempt you to resist this action.

Many of these forces may come from the psychopath himself, in the form of manipulative promises, dramatic gestures of contrition, or outright threats and other forms of abusive control. But many of them may also come internally, from within you—in the form of stubbornly clung-to hope, faith, the value of your fidelity to marital vows, your misgivings to break up your family, etc. You may feel scared to be alone again for many possible reasons, and after suffering so much indignity you may believe that this is your lot—that the *grass may be no greener* on the other side. Well, the grass is *much greener on the other side* of a psychopath, so long as you aren't drifting habitually to psychopathic partners as a pattern.

But let me stress what you absolutely should *not* do upon recognizing that your partner, or someone with whom you're closely involved, is psychopathic. You should *not* cling to false hope that he will meaningfully change. In contrast to "mutual funds," where "*past performance does not always ensure future, similar returns,"* with psychopaths *"past performance, behavior and attitudes are a virtual guarantee to persist in the future."* In a word, you can be certain that your investment in a psychopathic individual *will* produce disastrous future returns.

So...get out. Get away. *Stay* away. Get help to address the gravitational pull back. *Never* look back, other than with gratitude, and a feeling of accomplishment, that you chose to escape.

Chapter 23

WHEN PSYCHOPATHS BEHAVE NONPSYCHOPATHICALLY

There's a very good reason that psychopaths aren't always so easy to identify, and it's pretty simple—they aren't always behaving psychopathically. But that's not necessarily good news, as it leaves one at risk of interpreting the psychopath's "good behavior" as indicative of his potential to be a reliably good human being.

But as I wrote in a http://www.Lovefraud.com article, *"Bad Men Behaving Goodly,"* even the most destructive individuals aren't necessarily behaving badly 24/7. That's almost impossible. The very worst human beings have their better, seemingly more normal and humane moments.

Psychopaths can "look" very good and very normal, and can mask their underlying psychopathology sometimes very well--maybe even most of the time. But what we must never forget is the *fact* of their mentality—a mentality *always poised to scout and seize opportunities* to exploit others, regardless of how carefully, calculatingly, or impulsively they may exercise that inclination or impulse.

Therefore, I take some extra time to warn against perhaps the most enduring, persistent source of hope among those living with or loving a psychopathically inclined individual: "He is not *always* a scoundrel...not *always* manipulative, deceptive, or exploitative. He *can* be kind, nice, and giving—all the things I thought he was at his core."

And so yes, perhaps he can be these things or seem to be these things, perhaps even often. Perhaps, too, it's unnecessary to establish definitively whether the psychopath is *always simulating* these more *prosocial attitudes* when he's exhibiting them or whether, *selectively*, he is simply capable of being somewhat normal.

After all, he *is* human and it is his human side, or the *appearance* of it, that enables the disguise, or the submergence from visibility, of his psychopathy.

But one thing is certain, and bears repeating: the psychopath's prosociality will be a superficial dimension of his personality. At his *core*—as I've drummed incessantly throughout the book—he lacks a moral compass, a *conscience*, emotional depth, compassion, and anything approximating true maturity. Even when he is looking and behaving normally, his psychopathic orientation lies near, as in a state of *incubation*.

That is, just because he may not presently be actively exploiting *you* doesn't mean he's not exploiting someone *else*, or plotting to! Because it's almost certain that he is, or will be, sooner or later.

Chapter 24

WILL THE PSYCHOPATH INEVITABLY EXPLOIT HIS FAMILY?

think it bears noting that, while many psychopaths will wreck their families and exploit (and degrade) the trust of those who most rely on (and perhaps love) them, not all do, at least not directly.

This is where we get into the *compartmentalization* that psychopaths are chillingly capable of. The psychopath can sometimes lead a seemingly *normal family life* or *seemingly ordinary life*. It may be in his *"other life,"* or another sector of his life, that he is transgressing others psychopathically.

This means that not all psychopaths are *"acting out"* their psychopathy on those closest to them. But this does *not* mean that he's a psychopath toward his victims and nonpsychopathic toward his nonvictims.

The psychopath is a psychopath *all the time*, even if he's *not* exhibiting his psychopathy *all the time*. He is *psychopathic* because (with the psychopathic mentality we've been exploring) he victimizes and exploits *anyone*, not because he doesn't exploit and victimize *everyone*.

This last assertion is important. A bank robber is a bank robber if he robs *any* bank, not because he doesn't rob *every* bank. He may have reasons for selecting the particular banks he chooses to rob, and when. Some banks will be too risky to rob (most, in fact, will). The bank robber doesn't want his cover blown, so he'll be careful to target *vulnerable banks*. In the end, his selectiveness will be totally self-serving, just as the *psychopath's selection of his targets* will be predicated on self-serving factors.

The psychopath doesn't want his cover blown anymore than the bank robber. For the psychopath his family may even serve as a covering shield for his illicit, extracurricular psychopathic agenda. An apparently stable, normal family life can lessen suspicions around him, leaving him more latitude to express his psychopathy in moonlighting, alternate dimensions of his life.

Chapter 25

CHARISMATIC, MESMERIZING PSYCHOPATHS

Not all psychopaths are charismatic, mesmerizing personalities, and some are far from it; charisma is not a defining, necessary characteristic of the psychopath. Still, some psychopaths—a significant subset of them—possess what might be called a mesmerizing charisma. And much has been written about this fascinating psychopathic type.

If you think about it, if you take someone with a charismatic personality and endow him with psychopathic traits, then look out! That is just a highly dangerous combination. Charisma alone? Fantastic. But charisma conjoined with a philosophy that *whatever I want, I will take it*, with a vacant conscience? *That* is dangerous.

Charismatic psychopaths can sell you the shirt off *your* back. Why? Because in many respects they engender a kind of awe. Combine a fearless, audacious personality, endow him with a boatload of charm, *off-the-charts* seductiveness, a gift for glibness, extraordinary persuasiveness, and confidence exuding from his pores, and, depending on who you are, you are likely to *fall under the spell* of such an unusual individual. This *is* charisma personified.

The Psychopath's "Love Bombing"

A very dangerous form of the psychopath's display of his mesmerizing charisma is reflected in a behavior that has been called "love bombing." This is how the charismatic psychopath *deploys his charisma* to seduce someone he's targeting. There are excellent descriptions of love bombing in other books, such as in Donna Andersen's *Red Flags of Love Fraud: 10 Signs You're Dating a Sociopath*, and Claudia Moscovici's *Dangerous Liaisons: How To Recognize And Escape From Psychopathic Seduction*.

Basically, love bombing is the psychopath's strategy of setting his tentacles into his next conquest's heart with overwhelming levels of flattering, seductive attention. He "bombs" her with his *seemingly* loving solicitations.

Deep down all of us crave with a primitive, if dormant, intensity to be loved, idealized, and found irresistibly attractive, the more so by someone we find extremely, disarmingly attractive ourselves.

This a deep-seated fantasy—a fantasy, pursued or not, that often lies dormant and susceptible to awakening by a deft, manipulative puppeteer (in a word, a charismatic psychopath) who can activate its deeply, powerfully addicting qualities.

Charismatic psychopaths are often adept at love bombing their targets into heady stupefaction, leaving them believing they've found their *"soulmate,"* their *"once-in-a-lifetime love"*--that seemingly perfect man who, somehow, has fallen madly in love with, and is madly in devotion to, them. It is an *ominous sign to feel this way in the context of being love bombed.*

When you feel you are being "swept off your feet" and "treated like a queen" with an overwhelming burst of flattering, seductive attention, this is a sign you may be dealing with a manipulative personality who is targeting you to exploit in any number of possible alarming ways.

Charismatic psychopaths best meet the textbook image of psychopaths—smooth-talking con men who can convince you of anything. In general, professions or pursuits that encourage, if not require, high volumes of wheeling and dealing, brinksmanship, and gamesmanship will have a particular allure for the charismatic psychopath, who seeks thrill, risk, and acquisition.

This isn't to suggest that psychopaths won't be represented in all professions, blue- and white-collar, because they will. It's merely to suggest that your prototypical, charismatic psychopath will likely be drawn to professions that afford him opportunities to flex his manipulative, deceptive, glib inclinations.

Cult leaders are almost always charismatic psychopaths, some of them with comorbid (additional) psychiatric disorders as well. But cult leaders embody the traits of the charismatic psychopath. They are snake oil salesman with defunct consciences. Many televangelists are charismatic psychopaths, preying on the vulnerability and belief of deeply religious people, masquerading as "agents of God" possessed of special healing powers, while fleecing their congregants of money becomes their true "special calling."

Charismatic psychopaths exude a quality of supreme confidence, whose effect we will consider in the next chapter.

Chapter 26

Supremely Confident Psychopaths

I n the prior chapter we reviewed the charismatic psychopath's profile, which entails what I see as the psychopath's tendency to exude a supreme confidence. This is clearly true of the charismatic psychopath, and somewhat true of psychopaths in general. As always, there are exceptions—indeed many, to this generality—therefore it's *not* the case that someone can be *ruled out as psychopathic* for failing to exude this confidence.

But as a rule the psychopath is a low-fear, high-risk-seeking individual. Furthermore, when he wants something, as we now know so well, he is *undeterred by the harm he will cause others* to snatch it. This leaves him with a feeling of great inner protection against guilt (which he lacks), and against the chastening worry over the anticipated consequences of his exploitative agenda. This makes the psychopath, as we've described, *a very brazen, audacious personality.*

The psychopath's brazen audacity is typically experienced as his supreme confidence. And so we return to an important point made above—supreme confidence can be enormously persuasive and powerful. In the hands of an exploitative individual, supremely exuded confidence is a dangerous weapon.

What renders us often susceptible to another's supremely exuded confidence?

Because most of us carry self-doubt and are prone to thinking about "what ifs?" and worrying consequences to our actions, and because most of us are in touch with and perhaps more inhibited than we'd like to be by our vulnerability, we can find it disarming, exciting, and reassuring to be in the presence of someone seemingly so certain about himself, so self-assured, and so unflappable--in a word, someone who resonates supreme confidence.

How do you measure the integrity of a *seemingly* supremely confident individual? How can you know whether it's the confidence of a manipulative con man—a confidence turbo-charged by a missing conscience—or that of a truly grounded individual respectful of your boundaries? The deeply unsatisfying answer is that it can be awfully difficult.

But forgive me for returning to an earlier—but in this case, applicable—observation worth restating. When someone leaves you feeling exhilarated or spellbound, or when you find (against your instincts) that your guard, rather than gradually softening from exposure to an accumulation of trusting interactions and experiences, instead seems to be melting under the spell of an "entrancing other," it's a good idea to step back and ask yourself—what is happening here?

Is a manipulation of emotions occurring here? Am I dealing with someone who seems *in a hurry to accomplish or establish something* with me? Someone who seems *unusually determined to convince me of something sooner than I'm naturally convincible?* Someone who seems to be *blowing me away*, or seems to want to *blow away* or dispel my resistance? If the answer to any of these questions is yes, or *possibly* yes, caution is advised.

Chapter 27

For the Psychopath, The World As a Game

We've already established that not all psychopaths are smooth-talking, charming textbook types. There are paranoid psychopaths with menacing presentations, and socially unskilled psychopaths who, upon first impression, might barely *leave* an impression.

But it's important to reinforce this point—the psychopath, in general, is an envelope-pushing personality, a *game player* who tends to think along the lines, "*What* can I get away with? *Can* I get away with this? *How* can I get away with this? *Is* this something I can pull off?"

And in his grandiosity, his answer to the latter question will usually be *yes*.

The psychopath possesses great, if unwarranted, confidence in his insuperable powers to effectively scheme any agenda. Where most of us contemplating risky actions think, *"I don't think so. I'm not so sure this is a good idea,"* the psychopath will tend to think, with a glint in his eye, *"Sure, I can handle this. I can swing this. There's no reason I can't."* (This is illustrative of the supreme confidence to which we just alluded.)

Psychopaths tend to *size people up* and evaluate their *targetability*. This is the psychopath as watchful and predatory. Sometimes, in the presence of a psychopathically oriented individual, one can "feel" oneself being watched. This experience can evoke discomfort and can be a "red flag."

The "psychopathic stare" is a term denoting what has sometimes been observed as the invasive, intense, predatory watchfulness of some psychopaths. While not all psychopaths have "psychopathic eyes," calculating psychopaths, who may be assessing your vulnerability or evaluating in real time the success of their intended effect on you, may leave you feeling watched or studied with a disconcerting intensity.

In a dating situation, this could take the form of a psychopath's watching you with a seductive intensity that, as we noted earlier, can "feel" simultaneously flattering *and* uncomfortable. The psychopath, in these instances, is deploying a form of love bombing while evaluating his effect on you with his prying eyes.

In my clinical practice, I've had several experiences with psychopathic individuals who aren't merely glib but *prematurely glib* at the outset of an initial meeting. On the surface their persiflage may seem good-humored and ingratiating, but its prematurity, as noted earlier, can feel invasive. It feels "too soon," as if the individual doesn't know me well enough, or my sense of humor well enough, to know if this kind of verbal jousting will go over well with me. The "wise guy" surfaces immediately, and the immediacy feels "off."

What feels off is the sense that a boundary has been violated with a certain audacity. One feels the individual's indifference to the discomfort his liberties may cause. In fact, he is playing a certain game—his superficial congeniality and banter bely an *agenda* to test boundaries and his prospects to "get over" on you.

When this kind of glib intrusiveness is driven neither by anxiety or a social skills disorder, nor by an intellectual deficit, it can suggest a psychopathically manipulative origin. It can be very telling and very diagnostic.

Psychopaths exhibit some of their most blatant gamesmanship tendencies when *cornered to account* for their transgressions. Let's look a bit more probingly into this.

Chapter 28

CORNERED PSYCHOPATHS AND PSYCHOPATHIC LYING

Psychopaths are liars. They are chronic liars, and they are unrepentant liars. Some are good liars, and some less good, but lying comes easily to them, as do other variants of lying, like prevaricating, evading, and deceiving. For most psychopaths, the game of "getting over" on others, a theme I've driven home repeatedly, is a central component of their mentality.

When psychopaths are cornered, they will often lie. They will often lie even in the *glaring light of the exposure of their transgressions*, which is a particularly psychopathic form of lying. For many psychopaths, this can be a *virtual sport*—that is, evading detection and accountability, and relishing the opportunity to summon their *"inner Houdini"* to finagle their way out of *tight squeezes*.

Psychopaths can find it challenging and amusing to *talk their way* of jams, and more glib psychopaths can harbor enormous confidence in their ability to convince the greatest skeptic of their innocence.

Psychopaths are often storytellers and embellishers, capable of inventing fantastic explanations for behaviors that can be explained solely by virtue that they are psychopaths and behaving like psychopaths. In short, the *more cornered he is*, the more the psychopath will display his distinct aversion to—his apparent inability to—account for his actions.

I share an incident in my personal life that occurred about thirty years ago, an experience I had with someone who, surely, was highly psychopathic at a time when I knew little about psychopathy. But this real-life experience illustrates remarkably well how the psychopath operates.

As it happens, this was a female in her early twenties with whom I'd spent some time getting casually acquainted before I, with a group of others, left the apartment in which we were hanging out for a local club. This woman and I had been chatting for a while and seemingly had made a nice connection before we left.

On entering the crowded club, her friend (someone I'd also just met) approached me and warned me, "Be careful, she's a liar." To say the least, I found this warning to be disarming and confusing, for obvious reasons; but I recollect shrugging it off, lacking either the interest and/or convenient opportunity to probe it. (For all I knew this "friend" was dubious, *not* the woman she was warning me about.)

I had a hundred-dollar bill in my wallet—my only cash. This young woman and I were standing together, having (upon entering the club) somewhat naturally, casually "coupled off." I asked her what she wanted to drink, and she told me; she asked me what I wanted, and I told her. For some reason, she insisted on getting the drinks, so I handed her my bill and awaited her return. Five or ten minutes later, with no sign of her, I grew suspicious, her friend's warning now suddenly assuming a possible relevance.

Shortly I began snaking my way through the dense crowd to find her; before long I saw her standing in a distant corner with another guy, drink in hand. Amazed, I approached her and calmly, but firmly, asked her for my change. (I should add, incidentally, that upon entering the club minutes earlier, she was neither drunk nor drug-impaired, but sober and lucid.)

Without blinking an eye, to the best of my distinct memory, she answered me unflappably, "I don't know what you're talking about." I said something like, "Yes you do. I gave you a hundred-dollar bill to buy two drinks. You owe me the change. I want it." Again, looking me *squarely in the eye*, betraying *not the least bit of anxiety or uneasiness*, with an *expression of utter indifference* and detachment I recall vividly thirty years later, she answered something like, "I don't know what you're talking about it. You didn't give me anything."

Now I knew very well, immediately, that if I wasn't an expert on psychopathy back then, I was dealing with a clearly disturbed person with whom I had no leverage to reason or threaten. In retrospect, I was having an encounter, most certainly, with a psychopath. I had given her cash, but couldn't prove anything. She had bought herself a drink with my money, decided not to buy me the drink I requested, decided to pocket the considerable change and blow me off and seek interaction with another guy, and then deny that I ever gave her money. Moreover, as if that wasn't brazen enough, she claimed not to even recognize me when I approached and confronted her—that is, denying any prior contact we'd had.

Although I've sat with quite a few psychopathic individuals in the last twenty-five years, many in clinical settings, this personal experience, brief and nontraumatic as it ultimately was, still strikes me as incredibly illustrative of the psychopathic mentality in operation.

Let's look at some of the psychopathic qualities she exhibited. She was a liar and a particularly psychopathic liar. That is, *cornered and confronted directly with her freshly executed transgression*, she *calmly lied* with absolute composure. Nor was she lying from *shame*, but rather from *shamelessness*.

Lying from shamelessness, not shame, is a highly psychopathic form of lying.

Psychopaths are not squirmy, fidgety liars, as many nonpsychopaths are. When they look you in the face and lie, often there are no signs of *agitation* present, because there is no inner shame or guilt to agitate them.

In this case, this woman had an opportunity to steal my money. It's possible she'd groomed me for the opportunity with her prior attention to me, but it's also possible that her theft was relatively impulsive—that the opportunity simply presented itself and, recognizing it, she seized it.

In either case, she wanted my money, and *because she wanted it* (being highly psychopathic) she *took it* from me, *heedless of the harmfulness* of her violation.

Staying consistent with current themes, this woman *toyed* with me and was playing *games*, as psychopaths will do. She pretended I gave her no money, *because she could* (I couldn't prove it). She pretended she didn't recognize me, *because she could* (I couldn't prove it).

Although it's true that I couldn't enter her mind, I infer that she committed this act of exploitation with no guilt or compunction. After all, it would be impossible to perpetrate such a brazen, contemptuous, exploitative act with an active conscience. Furthermore, she subsequently had ample opportunity (had she "located" a conscience) to track me down, apologize, and return my money. But she didn't.

Empathy was missing, of course. But we've established that what really establishes *psychopaths as psychopaths* is less missing empathy per se, than a *pattern of missing empathy in the context of their conscious exploitation and violation of others.*

Although her exploitation of me posed little practical risk to her, what she did was breathtakingly audacious and consistent with the kind of jaw-dropping reactions psychopaths elicit.

After all, she knew that I'd be approaching her to account, yet was unconcerned. I was a sucker to her—as soon as she had my money, I was *useless* to her. Now, flush with ninety dollars cash, she could roam the floor for other guys. She must also have anticipated that I'd approach her friend and relate to the friend (who'd warned me) what happened. Furthermore, she appeared *shameless* to be accused of her thievery in front of the young man she'd begun engaging in conversation. None of these considerations ruffled her equanimity whatsoever.

Incidentally, let me tell you what she wasn't—while quietly personable and reserved, she was not charming, charismatic, seductive, or glib. I observe this to remind ourselves that, coming in all personality types, not all psychopaths will overwhelm us with charm, glibness, and charisma.

It's interesting how this personal anecdote really stuck with me. In retrospect, it was very informative. While it's true that assertions of the ubiquity of psychopaths may be somewhat hyperbolic, it's still the case that there have always been, and always will be, enough psychopathic individuals out there to make it a virtual certainty that, at various points or other, all of us will run across these individuals in our personal lives. The luckiest of us merely won't be devastated by our encounters with them.

Chapter 29

PSYCHOPATHS AND SEX

Bearing in mind the psychopath's *pushing-the-envelope*, *flouting-the-rules*, transgressive mentality, an *unencumbered-by-guilt, unaccountable mentality*—a mentality further characterized by low fear and a proclivity for risk—it should come as no big surprise that many psychopaths can *experience* and *use sex* with an aim to *feeling and producing big thrills and effects!*

As always, we don't want to overgeneralize. Not all psychopaths are highly sexual individuals or sexual wave-makers. Not all psychopaths will distinguish themselves one way or another, sexually. Thus, even in the sexual sphere, it's important not to caricature or pigeonhole the psychopath's presentation.

Still, as we bear his mentality in mind, we can appreciate why many psychopaths, especially in the course of *grooming a target*, will seek to *"make the sex memorable"* as a means of hooking or snagging the object of his sexual agenda. For such psychopaths, the *delivery of great sex* is a game and challenge he may actively seek.

Psychopaths, then, can be thrilling sexual partners if their aim, in fact, is to thrill, seduce, and captivate. The psychopath, as we know, when love bombing can leave you feeling very special, and sometimes very sexually special. It's also true that some psychopaths, with an awareness that something is deeply missing in their personalities, see the opportunity to deliver a memorable sexual experience as a compensatory means to hook their prey. The sexualized psychopath uses sex manipulatively and seductively. Of course, the flip side is much darker; the psychopath can be sexually degrading and abusive because, at bottom, he will relate to you as a sexual object.

Let us not forget—you exist to entertain and satisfy *him*. Thus, it might entertain *him* to entertain *you*, in which case, to the best of his ability, he may want to leave you feeling swoons of rapture. Conversely, it might entertain him to *degrade and abuse you, or otherwise leave you feeling humiliated*. Regardless, *his entertainment* will supersede everything.

It goes without saying that to be left, ever, feeling degraded in *any* arena, including the sexual, is sufficient grounds to *exit stage left* immediately, with no looking back and no second chances proffered. But it's also worth invoking an earlier observation: while not necessarily proof of something amiss, still the experience, *any* experience, of feeling overwhelmed, mesmerized, *totally blown away*, and captivated, including sexually— such an experience itself can signify that something is amiss. The something that *felt* "unreal"—giddily, intoxicatingly unreal—may in fact *have* been.

Or it may be more accurate to suggest that, sometimes, such overwhelming, captivating, incredibly exciting experiences may have been "real," while the *deliverer of these experiences* may *not* have been.

In some respects this captures the slippery, seductive, dangerous enigma of the charismatic psychopath. While capable of delivering *"Oh my God,"* jaw-dropping experiences that *feel* very real, *he* really is not.

Chapter 30

The Psychopath as *Wizard of Oz*

The psychopath in many respects is a real-life *Wizard of Oz*—an effect creator lacking substance, a master of special effects, an impression-maker, an emotional simulator, and a string-puller.

There is no personality profile and no mentality in all the world that conceals beneath his engaging veneer the gaping hollowness of the psychopath.

When I think of *The Wizard of Oz*, I think of the psychopath, metaphorically living his life *as if* behind a *psychological screen*, pulling the levers of his powers in bemused secrecy, observing with contemptuous amusement the effects on others of his machinations, reveling in his powers to dupe, control, and manipulate those "dumb enough" to *allow themselves* to be violated.

If, as an experiment, you could give children the magical powers, behind a one-way mirror, to manipulate the actions and reactions of adults in a room, to make the adults do what the children dictated, and to make the adults react the way the children secretly directed them to, the children would likely find that to be a quite exhilaratingly fun experiment. As a matter of fact, let's be honest: if, in the same experiment, you gave a group of normal adults similar magical powers to effect, secretly, in a group of *unaware adults*, behind a one-way mirror, the reactions and actions they directed, those superempowered adults *behind the mirror* might find their secret powers to be almost as fascinating, perhaps as entertaining, as the children would find them. And there is nothing abnormal or unhealthy about any of this. These would be relatively normal reactions among the *experimentally empowered* group.

However, in the *real world*, even *if* imbued with these hypothetical powers, the adults would quickly develop *ambivalent feelings* about them. The *non*psychopathic adults quickly would begin to question, if nothing else, their comfort level with (and their "rights" to use) such powers. They would view such powers, or superpowers, at the very least with caution—*not* as licensing them, with no compunction, to exploit others' boundaries, secretly, merely because they can.

They would not view others as "suckers" and "fools" merely because others would be susceptible to their machinations should they elect to exercise them. After their flirtation with the mischievous use of their omnipotence, they would quickly realize that their responsibility is *not* to violate others' dignity and boundaries, even if others are violable.

Now, children are another story. Being less emotionally mature, and with their values and consciences less fully formed, they might extend these experimental powers into the "real world," and exercise them for a longer stretch of time, and with less compunction, than the adults in our experiment would. They are children, after all. The children might take their powers *out of the experimental setting* and extend them into the real world, continuing to find it fun, even hilarious, to watch themselves effecting and eliciting behaviors from others who are obliviously receptive to their manipulative dictates. They would watch themselves, and enjoy watching themselves, inducing others to compromise themselves unwittingly.

I believe that psychopaths possess this basic mentality to a great extent. They are like the children in our experiment, perceiving themselves, rightly or not, to possess these magical powers. Because they perceive themselves to possess them, they perceive themselves to *have the right* to exercise them.

A mind-boggling contempt for others' dignity characterizes their worldview, which reflects something like, "If you are *dumb enough* to be vulnerable to my machinations, that's *your* problem, because *my* entertainment and *my* gratification are infinitely more important than any cost *you* incur in supplying them!"

In this sense, the psychopath is fixated at a very early level of emotional/moral development. But this might be a charitable, even inaccurate, depiction of his developmental status. Even normal young children show remarkable evidence of empathy and compassion that psychopaths are missing, suggesting deficits that go even deeper than mere questions of developmental arrest.

But I stray, for the moment. I suggested the psychopath is a sort of *Wizard of Oz*. But he is not entirely so; the analogy is apt only to a certain extent. For the psychopath, fundamentally, does not engage in his deceptions, his artifices, his pretenses, and his false personas principally from insecurity, anxiety, or the classical experience of "feeling small" and, thereby, compensatorily needing to "feel big."

If this were the case, there might be hope. Self-esteem issues would be the primary factors driving his pathological attitudes and behaviors. But this is not the case. The psychopath may possess insecurities, as all of us do. But his insecurities, wherever they may lie, do not begin to explain his psychopathic personality. The latter is better understood as a function *not* of his misguidedly expressed vulnerability, but rather his seemingly programmed compulsion to exploit vulnerability.

Chapter 31

The Psychopath's Corrupt, Rogue Mentality

The psychopath's is a corrupt, rogue mentality. Take such a mentality, infuse it with high levels of grandiosity and a deep contempt for others' dignity, and you are homing in on very core elements of psychopathy.

I don't know that psychopathy is often characterized as a *disorder of psychological corruption*. But I think it should be, because the psychopath is a deeply, immutably, *psychologically corrupt individual*. How, precisely, is he corrupt? Of course, we've discussed this through the book and know the answer to this question by now. But it's always smart to review core questions.

No person, no system, and no set of rules or laws should obstruct the psychopath who, as we know, tends to feel somewhat omnipotent in his capacity to *circumvent all obstacles* in his path. Why? Because he believes he is *smarter and cleverer* than others, and perhaps more powerful, but most importantly, he believes he has the *right to exploit* his *perceived comparative advantages* over others.

And so we return, yet again, to a core point. The psychopath regards *his* needs and gratifications as *infinitely more important* than others'. *His* needs and gratifications *always trump the dignity and security* of others'.

When I call the psychopath's a rogue mentality, I refer to the blatant contempt he has for the concept of limits. As we've discussed at length, the psychopath *rejects* limits. He is *affronted* by limits and has no use for them; they are inconveniences and hindrances to him, to be trodden and eliminated as obstructions in his path.

In whatever forms—whether as rules, laws, physical barriers, or interpersonal barriers—the psychopath has *contempt for what limits him*. He is an eliminator of limits. The violent psychopath will eliminate *you* if you stand in his way.

This is what I mean when I call psychopaths "rogue." Let me illustrate some psychopathic, rogue thinking. If a psychopath was to spot a misplaced wallet on a crowded train platform through a maze of legs at rush hour and wanted the money and credit cards he imagined inside the wallet, his thinking might go like this: *"Hey, there's a wallet on the platform over there, just lying there, people are stepping right over it, nobody sees it! Some **sucker** left it there. Ha! There's probably money and credit cards in it. I'm pretty broke. This may be my lucky day! Now, let me **plow through these idiots** who are **in my way** before someone else grabs the fucking wallet! What are the chances someone will bust me stealing the wallet? None! And even if I'm busted, who can prove I wasn't gonna return it?? Ha! Jesus, I will **knock these idiots onto the fucking tracks** if I have to, because they are **in my way**, the morons. Fucking move, morons, **get the fuck out of my way**…There it is. I can't believe it, a fucking wallet just sitting there. Now let's hope there's something in it, because if there isn't, I'm gonna be pissed off…I'm gonna be pissed off, if this is just some fucking tease."*

In my experience with psychopathic-minded personalities, this *train of thought* typifies their corrupted, rogue perspective, containing most of its elements. If you don't recognize yourself in these *trains of thought*—if you find their boldness, audacity, preoccupation with self-gratification, and jaw-dropping contempt of others' boundaries and dignity hard to relate to personally— then I've got some sobering news for you: you are *low in psychopathic traits and tendencies.* You just aren't anything close to psychopathic.

If you saw a wallet being trampled on a crowded train platform in the madness of a rush-hour commute, but took the view that it doesn't belong to you but to the individual who lost it, and chose not to seize it for that reason or to seize it with the intention of returning it to its owner, because you believe you aren't entitled to the things you might like to have and *could take* but that don't belong to you—if this is your perspective, then let me tell you something: you would be something of a fool, a dope, really something of a wuss *in the eyes of a psychopath*.

Chapter 32

ARE PSYCHOPATHS EVERYWHERE?

Yes and no. Let me explain. Contrary to what Martha Stout would have you believe in *The Sociopath Next Door*, her sensationalized account of psychopaths, they are not swarming around us like flies. As we noted earlier, probably less than 1 percent of the general population is seriously psychopathic, and so the likelihood that your neighbor is a psychopath, while certainly possible, is pretty slim.

And so it's important to keep this perspective in mind. Most people are not psychopaths. Indeed, the vast majority of individuals are not seriously, dangerously psychopathic. Yet enough *are* that it becomes extremely important to be knowledgeable about these individuals.

In a sense it's that simple. If one in a hundred, or one in a hundred and twenty, or one in a hundred and fifty people are seriously psychopathic, it is statistically highly probable that you will have encounters with psychopaths, periodically, throughout your life, because while they may represent a relatively small portion of the general population *percentage-wise*, still their percentage representation is not *so small as to be anything close to rare*. Factor in the enormity of the general population, and we are left inescapably to conclude that a great many psychopathic individuals really do exist and are out and about. Inevitably we will be crossing paths with them at various points in our lives, hopefully (if we're lucky) not as targets of their psychopathic machinations.

A knowledge of the psychopath—a good understanding of what makes him tick—can possibly raise our internal awareness, freshen our red flag alert system to his presence and, while offering no guaranteed protection, perhaps lower our vulnerability and susceptibility to his exploitative intentions.

Chapter 33

Just a Jerk, or a Psychopath?

Let's revisit this question from a different angle. Earlier, I suggested that psychopathy, like so many conditions and disorders, is located on a continuum. One can possess zero to few traits of psychopathic personality, up the scale to more traits and relatively higher locations on the psychopathic continuum, at which point, high enough up on the continuum, we begin to designate an individual as pretty seriously, if not outright, psychopathic.

As noted, Robert Hare, Ph.D. has developed arguably the most sophisticated psychometric tools for rating psychopathy levels in individuals. But even Hare's tools are somewhat arbitrary. He has cut-off scores, you'll remember, above which he designates someone as psychopathic, below which, point by decreasing point, he calls them relatively less psychopathic.

Still, Hare himself has suggested that just because a score of thirty to forty on his adult psychopathy measurement gets you a designation "psychopath," scores just below thirty, or above twenty, still suggest significant psychopathic tendencies and render one someone to be wary of, at the very least. Is there really a significant difference between an individual scoring a twenty-nine on Hare's scale versus a thirty or thirty-one?

Is the thirty really a psychopath and the twenty-nine or twenty-eight not? Yes, it really *is* the case that most everything is relative and must be appreciated as such. Still, I think it's worth stressing that psychopathic thinking really is quite unique, quite clear-cut, quite hard-core thinking in many respects. It's not normal thinking. Psychopathic individuals, when targeting a gratification to pursue, really tend to think in the *psychopathic ways* we've elaborated throughout the book.

In this sense, they are very different from your garden-variety "jerk." A jerk may behave badly, which can make him a jerk, but even if he's a *real jerk*, he's going to *feel badly* about hurting you when he learns he's hurt you. He may not feel badly in the moment, but most likely he eventually will when he's had time to realize he was a jerk. Then, most likely, he's going to want to make amends from a true—not just manipulative—desire to do so.

A jerk may *want what he wants*, but is unlikely to exploit you unconscionably. He may act selfishly, even *be* selfish, but unlike the psychopath, who reacts indifferently to the casualties he leaves in the wake of his violating incursions into others' lives, the jerk won't.

A jerk is someone who, in a lousy mood that he's mismanaging, cuts you off recklessly on the road and, seeing in his rearview mirror that his maneuver caused a fender bender, stops his car and, feeling lousy, embarrassed, and scared, goes to check to see if everyone is all right, prepared to take the heat, if not responsibility. A psychopath is someone who cuts you off recklessly, and, seeing that his daredevil action caused a fender bender, flees the scene. Flees it *thinking*, perhaps even *laughing* to himself, "Woah…shit. *That* was funny." Or, "That's not *my* problem, people can't fucking drive." Or, "Damn, I better get the fuck out of here, nobody will know I had anything to do with it…*My* car's fine, not a scratch on it. *See ya*, suckers! Good luck with your insurance!"

Psychopaths, I can't stress enough, possess a *truly frightening level of contempt*, something approaching a privately felt mirth over what they can get away with. Jerks don't revel in their capacity to "get over" on others like psychopaths do. The psychopath sees others as just so stupid, so naive, so vulnerable, and so *exploitable* it's *almost funny*, while perceiving *himself* to be just so smart, so canny, so clever, and so adept at playing the system and playing people it's *almost funny*.

Speaking of funny, I've been asked: do psychopaths have a sense of humor? A real sense of humor? Unfortunately, yes—meaning, the psychopath's condition doesn't necessarily preclude his having a sense of humor or capacity to be funny. As I just noted, many psychopaths can find humor in a great many things, including their abuse and exploitation of others. Unfortunately, then, possessing a sense of humor or being funny doesn't rule one out as a psychopath.

Now being involved with a jerk isn't necessarily the wisest decision to make, but then jerks, like everyone else, also come in degrees. Moreover, most of us, at our worst, can be jerks. But as simplistic as this sounds, a jerk, when he's done being a jerk, will care about you. As I suggested, when he gets over himself your typical jerk, who's not much more than that, will want to make things better with some authenticity. When he sees what he's damaged or wrecked, he is likely to shudder and think something like, *"Oh Jesus, what have I done… again?"* Or, *"Oh my God, I really messed up…I've got some repairing to do."*

The psychopath does not look at the wreckage he's caused and think with dismay, *"I had no right to do that.*

*Man, I really fucked up. I just had no right to do that. Wow, I need to make amends **because I had no right to do that.***"

Let me repeat this, because I think it's pretty critical. The psychopath will never seek to make amends from the dismaying thought, *"I had no right to do that."* Any *amend seeking* he pursues will be motivated *principally to reinstate a more comfortable existence for himself.*

Chapter 34

PSYCHOPATHS AND THEIR CULPABILITY

Psychopathy, to be clear, is not a legal defense—psychopaths are *legally culpable* for their criminally psychopathic behaviors, even though their *psychopathic condition* arguably destines them to perpetrate their transgressions.

If psychopathy truly arises from *deficits the psychopath can't help*, isn't it fair, at least, to question whether he should be held accountable for the *harm his condition assures he will cause?* Moreover, if his condition is untreatable, if he really can't be helped (as is true), and if his disorder is impervious to intervention (as it true), isn't it fair, at least, to question whether this should decrease his liability for the harm he causes?

From my perspective, the answer to these questions is, "No."

The psychopath *should be held totally accountable* for his transgressions. I refer to *non*mentally retarded, *non*psychotic psychopaths—which is to say, *intellectually intact* psychopaths whose "reality testing" is not significantly impaired by another mental illness.

The *intellectually intact* psychopath is a fascinating conundrum—intellectually he *knows* what he is doing, *knows* he is violating and transgressing others.

Alluding to our earlier, hypothetical scenario, when he covets and targets a wallet to steal, he *knows* it doesn't belong to him and, *intellectually*, knows he has no *true right* to it. When he invades a woman's space and gropes her, and thinks it's funny and amusing, he isn't suffering from Asperger's syndrome, "lost in space" with truly no intellectual and/or spacial sense of proper boundaries. He *knows* intellectually that others do not want to be groped, and that to grope others is likely to leave them feeling highly uncomfortable if not frightened and disturbed.

He knows it's *considered wrong* to steal the wallet and *considered wrong* to grope the woman but does it anyway. Why? Mainly—and we have to keep returning to this point—because he *wants to*. Because there is *something in it* for him. And that is sufficient, that there is something *in it* for him. Contemplating the cost to others of his actions and *caring about that cost* (as we've emphasized throughout) is missing in his calculus.

We've entered the psychopath's mind at various points and learned that how he *takes things apart* is neither terribly complicated nor unpredictable, after all. He thinks, as our prior examples have demonstrated, things like, "I *want* that…What I'm about to do may be *considered* wrong, but I'm going to *do* it anyway, and why? Because it *looks fucking gratifying* to me. Now let me ask myself a big question? Can I can *pull this off?* Sure, I'm not so worried about that. As far as there being victims? Hey…we're all *victims of something* or someone, right? If you can't protect *yourself* in this cold, harsh world, that's *your* problem. Learn how! Ha ha. Meanwhile, lemmee snatch that wallet out of that loser's pocket because he looks rich and besides, he's probably got more money than he knows what to do with. LOL. Let's do it."

If we were to further simplify psychopathic thinking, we might distill it to something like, *"Yeah, I know what I'm about to do is wrong…I know it will hurt someone…but at the end of the day, it's gonna feel good to me, real good, end of story."*

And so the psychopath *knows* but still *does*. Is psychopathy a compulsive disorder? I don't think so, not *primarily*. If it could be proven it is, perhaps this would further an argument for the psychopath's incompetence—his incompetence to be held to normal standards of law-abiding conduct. This isn't to suggest that psychopaths, for instance violent psychopaths such as even serial killers, aren't engaged in struggles with compulsive urges. Some serial killers have described their "demons" as exercising a sort of compulsive power over them felt as difficult, if not impossible, to resist.

But regardless of the extent to which compulsive processes can be found in certain expressions of psychopathic acting out, I'd still assert that *primarily what drives* the psychopath's condition isn't a compulsive mentality, but an empathetically, compassionately defunct one—a mentality that identifies, to say it a last time, "*I **want** that, so I'm gonna **take** it…Now, **get the hell out of my way,** and **let's make sure I don't get caught** doing this.*"

The most sensitive of us can feel sad, perhaps, for the psychopath and his quite morbid deficits. Perhaps an argument can be made to pity him, pity his emotional and psychological poverty. But in the end, although his is a disorder of a *perversely lacking accountability*, the psychopath must be held accountable. Like the rest of us with intact intellects and nonpsychotic minds, with various deficits strewn through our personalities and characters, the psychopath must be held responsible to behave well, even though we know he won't and, para-doxically, understand why he can't.

But when he doesn't—when he violates and trans-gresses—he must be held culpable. While true that he *can't help being* the most dangerous, menacing in-dividual that exists in the world, this just makes it extra-imperative that he pay the fullest price for his destructiveness.

Concluding Remarks

I hope very much that I achieved my aim with this book—to explain in a clear, interesting way just who the psychopath is, how he thinks, and what makes him tick. I hope you feel I succeeded? If you do, I'll express my gratitude again, in advance, for spreading the word about my book in any and all ways you can. And favorable Amazon reviews would be hugely appreciated.

Meanwhile, I invite you to read and subscribe to my blog *http://www.unmaskingthepsychopath.com*, where I'll continue exploring the fascinating world of psychopathic thinking and behavior with regular, illuminating posts.

I also invite your feedback, direct or indirect. I welcomed you with my contact information and depart, for now, leaving you with the same.

I can be e-mailed at powercommunicating@yahoo.com

My content-laden website is http://www.power-communicating.com

My cell phone is 1-908-456-2679.

I look forward to hearing from you.

Suggested Resources

There are many excellent books about psychopathy out there. I recommend three to explore for their especially trenchant insights into the subject.

Donna Andersen, author of *Red Flags of Love Fraud--10 Signs You're Dating A Sociopath*

Anderson is the founder of Lovefraud.com, a fantastic website dedicated to educating the public about psychopaths. She writes with great personal experience and wisdom about psychopathic personality.

Claudia Moscovici, author of *Dangerous Liaisons: How to Recognize and Escape from Psychopathic Seduction*.

Moscovici is a penetrating writer on psychopathy. Everything she writes is studded with insights. This book makes an invaluable contribution to the literature.

Moscovici also wrote *The Seducer*, a gripping novel that's as good as fiction gets on the subject.

Hervey Cleckley, author of *The Mask of Sanity*, was a pioneer in the study of psychopaths, and this book is an enduring classic and worth every penny you will pay in the used-book market for it. It is regrettable, if not inexplicable, that it's gone out of print.

22864192R00094

Made in the USA
San Bernardino, CA
24 July 2015